MATZO

MATZO

35 Recipes
for Passover *and*
All Year Long

Michele Streit Heilbrun
and David Kirschner

Photography by JENNIFER MAY

Clarkson Potter/Publishers
NEW YORK

MH:
For my Joey

DK:
*To all Kirschners past,
present, and future*

Published in the United States by Clarkson Potter/
Publishers, an imprint of the Crown Publishing Group, a
division of Penguin Random House LLC, New York
crownpublishing.com
clarksonpotter.com

CLARKSON POTTER is a trademark and POTTER with
colophon is a registered trademark of Penguin Random
House LLC

Library of Congress Cataloging-in-Publication Data
Names: Heilbrun, Michele Streit, author.
Title: Matzo : 35 recipes for Passover and all year
long / Michele Streit
   Heilbrun ; photographs by Jennifer May.
Description: First Edition. | New York : Clarkson
Potter, 2017.
Identifiers: LCCN 2016019497 (print) | LCCN
2016034215 (ebook) (print) |
   LCCN 2016034216 (ebook) | ISBN
9780804188999 (hardback) | ISBN
   9780804189002 (Ebook)
Subjects: LCSH: Passover cooking. |
Matzos. | BISAC: COOKING / Regional &
   Ethnic / Jewish & Kosher. | COOKING
/ Holiday. | COOKING / Specific
   Ingredients / General. | LCGFT:
Cookbooks.
Classification: LCC TX739.2.P37
H45 2017 (print) | LCC TX739.2.P37
(ebook) |
   DDC 641.5676437--dc23
LC record available at https://
lccn.loc.gov/2016019497

ISBN 978-0-8041-8899-9
eBook ISBN 978-0-8041-8900-2

Printed in China

Book and cover design by
Sonia Persad
Cover photography by
Jennifer May

First Edition
10 9 8 7 6 5 4 3 2 1

CONTENTS

INTRODUCTION . . . 6
THE HOLIDAY OF MATZO . . . 9

BREAKFASTS . . . 17

STARTERS . . . 31

SIDES
AND SNACKS . . . 47

ENTRÉES . . . 67

DESSERTS . . . 93

ACKNOWLEDGMENTS . . . 108
INDEX . . . 110

INTRODUCTION

Most Jews think about matzo only at Passover, when it appears on their seder table or in their matzo brei. For many, eating matzo is an annual event like the Fourth of July fireworks or the White Sale at Macy's—enjoyed while it's there, forgotten when it's gone. But things are different for me. Very different. I'm a Streit, which means matzo has been a vital part of my life every single day.

It's fair to say I was born into matzo—that it's in my DNA. It was, and still is, the family business, and it plays a starring role in my most cherished memories. Working the counter at my grandfather's factory, making change at the register while snacking on mandel toast, finding comfort from the warmth of the ovens—matzo is at the heart of all these memories. These scenes may not paint the extravagant life people associate with a "matzo heiress," but matzo isn't about extravagance. It's about tradition.

It all started with my great-grandfather Aron Streit. Aron was a baker in Austria. He arrived in America in the 1890s and immediately sensed a need for matzo in New York's enormous immigrant community. So he began making it by hand. As the business grew, he opened a factory on Manhattan's Lower East Side and brought his two sons, Jack and Irving, into the company.

Jack was my grandfather. Loud and ebullient, he loved being a Streit, but mostly he loved the factory. He worked there until he died at age ninety-one, every day adjusting the oven temperature ever so slightly to ensure the matzo was light, crisp, and perfect. You see, as proud as my family is of its Jewish identity, we're equally proud of our matzo.

Decades later, my cousins, fourth- and fifth-generation matzo makers, continue to run the business. Though the original factory on Rivington Street has since closed, the company has the same phone number, the iconic pink packaging remains, and

Our Rivington Street storefront circa 1980s.

the energy inside the factory is still frenetic—after all, if the matzo isn't made within eighteen minutes of water touching the flour, it's considered leavened, and for matzo makers, that's a *shanda*—a shame. But the world outside those walls is wildly different than it was when Aron first started baking. Everything has evolved, from technology to dating. Now, it's matzo's turn.

Matzo, with its ancient origins, is bursting with modern possibilities. I've known this since childhood. Its journey from the Passover table into everyday food is long overdue. Consider this cookbook matzo's makeover. It takes traditional Jewish recipes and ushers them into the alluring world of modern, innovative cooking. David Kirschner, seasoned chef, fellow food lover, and true mensch, has helped me breathe fresh air into classics and create new recipes that will dazzle your guests at Passover and beyond. The rich fragrance of Chicken-Stuffed Whole-Wheat Matzo Balls simmering gently in mushroom broth will make you *kvell*, and the tender crunch of our Matzo Spanakopita will have your friends and family begging for it year-round.

After thousands of years, matzo has finally arrived.

NOSH   eat, snack

THE HOLIDAY OF MATZO

If you're reading this book, there's a high likelihood you already know what we're doing here. The Passover yontif, *or holiday, happens every spring. It is the oldest Jewish festival that has been observed continuously, a tradition even longer than lighting the Hanukkah candles. But for you goys out there, here's a crash course.*

THE SEDER

Passover begins with the seder, a ceremonial and celebratory dinner celebration on the first and second nights of the holiday. It commemorates the Israelites' exodus from Egypt after being enslaved for four hundred years, oy! Using a prayer book called the Haggadah, the seder leads us through the story of how God rescued the Israelites from slavery. Everyone interprets the seder in their own way, but if you're lucky, yours will include songs, like the traditional *Dayenu*. But every version, fun or snoozy, will contain the following rituals:

THE SEDER PLATE

Shank Bone: Represents the lamb sacrificed on the eve of the Exodus from Egypt

Hard-boiled egg: Represents the offering that was brought in the days of the Holy Temple

Maror **(bitter herbs):** Represents the bitterness of slavery

Karpas **(fresh vegetable):** Usually parsley or boiled potato dipped in salt water, representing the tears of the slaves and a new beginning

Charoset **(sweet mixture of nuts, fruit, and wine):** Represents mortar, a reminder of the labor the Jews were made to do

*Chazeret***:** The second bitter herb, commonly romaine lettuce, which has the same meaning as the *maror*

ELIJAH'S CUP

Every seder table contains a cup of wine for Elijah the Prophet, a "guest" you hope will arrive one day to resolve all controversial questions of Jewish law. When determining how many cups of wine should be drunk during the seder, ancient rabbis couldn't decide whether that number should be four or five. Their solution was to drink four cups of wine and then pour another one for Elijah (the fifth cup). When he returns it will be up to him to decide whether this fifth cup should be consumed at the seder!

A newer tradition has Miriam's cup on the Seder table, too. This cup, filled with water, represents the role of Miriam the Prophetess in the exodus and symbolizes the contributions of women to Jewish culture.

THE FOUR QUESTIONS

Traditionally, the youngest child reads the four questions, to include the child(ren) in the Seder and to symbolize asking and seeking more to become free from internal constraints and reach a higher spiritual level.

- Why on all other nights do we eat bread or matzo, while on this night we eat only matzo?
- Why on all other nights do we eat all kinds of vegetables and herbs, but on this night we have to eat bitter herbs?
- Why on all other nights do we not dip our vegetables in salt water, but on this night we dip them twice?
- Why on all other nights do we eat while sitting upright, but on this night we eat while reclining?

THE MATZO PLATE

Three pieces of matzo are served on a separate plate, covered and separated by linen. These represent the three classes of Jewish people: the *Kohens* (priests), Levites (assistants in temple), and Israelites (everybody else). Early in the seder, the leader lifts the three matzos and breaks the middle piece in half. The larger of those halves is called the *afikomen*, which will be the ceremonial dessert of the seder. In some traditions, the kids try to steal the *afikomen* from the leader throughout the meal. In others, the piece of matzo is wrapped in a cloth and hidden in the home for the kids to find toward the end of the seder, often (and definitely in my family) for a prize.

Our classic five-pound box.

Of course, this is a very concise version of a seder. There is so much more: the Four Sons, the Ten Plagues, the kiddush (prayer over the wine), many more sips of wine, lighting candles, hand washing, and, of course, concluding with "Next Year in Jerusalem!" It is a beautiful, thoughtful celebration where we ask a lot of questions and contemplate our place in the world.

WHY THIS BOOK?

So, back to the matzo. The whole reason we are here! Even after the seder, the Passover holiday requires changing your diet for its eight-day duration. Jews remove *hametz* (food that is leavened) from their lives. It reminds us of the time the Jews were an enslaved people who did not have the luxury of waiting for their dough to rise as they were hastily led out of Egypt's desert by Moses.

We wanted to create an easy-to-use resource for ways to eat all that matzo. We felt the "bread of affliction" had gotten a bad rap! Sure, there are your classics, like brisket and matzo ball soup and matzo brei, but have you ever stopped to think about how many more delicious ways this cracker can be used? Don't worry—we have. We're excited to serve up our twist on everything we just mentioned, and

Observing the product

much more. Matzo Nachos? Yes, please. Stuffing? Don't mind if we do. And we couldn't imagine a better ending than an Apple Crumb Pie.

The level of observance of the holiday is a very personal choice, and laws and standards vary even within communities. Some people clean their houses and change over their dishes, not wishing to use anything that touched *hametz*, and some people simply avoid leavened products.

Everyday kosher means not mixing meat with dairy and eating foods that are prepared in a way that is approved by Jewish kosher guidelines. While eating kosher for Passover, one must avoid leavened bread, certain grains that ferment when mixed with water, and *kitniyot* (beans, peas, lentils, rice, corn, and legumes) in addition to all of the traditional kosher laws.

Some Ashkenazi Jews do not eat *kitniyot* on Passover, but many Sephardic Jews do.

Each recipe also indicates which non-Passover dietary category it fits into. You'll see indications alongside every recipe; here's what they mean:

Meat: Regular kosher meat is considered kosher for Passover, but it cannot be consumed with dairy. If you eat meat, the custom is to wait six hours before consuming dairy in order to stay kosher.

Dairy: Dairy is considered kosher for Passover, but cannot be consumed alongside meat. If you do have dairy, after washing out your mouth, you may eat meat after thirty minutes.

Parve: These are neutral foods that contain neither meat nor dairy. For this reason, parve foods can be consumed alongside meat or dairy foods.

Some recipes may contain additional explanation. The category that applies depends on your choice of ingredients—for example, if you use margarine instead of butter, it will be parve instead of dairy. This will be outlined for you.

THE PASSOVER PANTRY AND KITCHEN

Before you get started, what will you need? Many items that you regularly cook with can be used here. But you may need to stock up on certain ingredients to make the recipes kosher for Passover. Unless noted otherwise, you should be able to find everything in your supermarket. Let's take a look at what we'll be cooking with.

INGREDIENTS

Plain unsalted matzo: Needs no explanation.

Matzo meal: Matzo that has been coarsely ground. Matzo meal is found in a variety of our recipes like matzo balls, blintzes, tortillas, and fried chicken. It can also be used for thickening soups and for breading.

Matzo cake meal: Matzo that has been ground very fine, like flour. We use cake meal in a variety of our recipes: apple pie, pancakes, chocolate torte, and chocolate chip cookies.

Farfel: This is simply matzo broken into small, dime-sized pieces. Because of its size and density, it creates a lot of texture in foods like granola, braised chicken, stuffing, gratin, and Rocky Road Truffles.

Potato starch: A natural, dry starch made from potatoes that's used to thicken sauces and help bring a crunchy texture to baked goods.

Eggs: All of the recipes call for large eggs.

Salt: We like to use Diamond Crystal kosher salt. The saltiness of kosher salt brands varies, so remember to adjust your seasoning when using a different brand.

Pepper: We mean freshly ground black pepper.

Butter: Unless stated otherwise, we use unsalted butter, as we like to control the seasoning ourselves.

Unsalted margarine: This is a parve butter substitute made mostly of refined vegetable oil and water.

Schmaltz: The word is derived from Yiddish and means clarified chicken fat; sometimes it's seasoned with fried onions, too. Its flavor is incomparable for cooking, but you can always substitute vegetable oil. Schmaltz is available at most kosher butchers, but you can easily make your own (see page 32).

Herbs: We always use fresh, unless stated otherwise.

Citrus juice: We also prefer freshly squeezed juices.

Olive oil: Anytime we use it, it's extra virgin.

Neutral oil: A neutral oil is best for high-heat cooking. Cottonseed, grapeseed, walnut, and safflower oil are the best choices for Passover, as most others are considered *kitniyot*.

If you want to stay within the strict kosher guidelines, you can find many kosher for Passover products here:

https://oukosher.org/passover

http://www.crcweb.org

http://www.star-k.org

KITCHEN EQUIPMENT

Blender: An electric culinary appliance with a high-speed blade used to puree, chop, and liquefy in food preparation.

Food processor: Similar to a blender, the main difference is the interchangeable blades and attachments. Also, the bowl is shorter and wider and, unlike a blender, very little liquid is necessary for the processor to operate.

Thermometer: Used to check the doneness of food and ensure proper and safe internal temperatures. Some thermometers, like deep-fry and candy thermometers, clip onto the side of a pot and remain there throughout the cooking process while others are inserted near the end to check if the food is done.

Wire rack: Typically used to cool hot food. The rack allows air to circulate underneath, so food cools on all sides and doesn't become soggy.

Hand mixer: Lightweight handheld mixing device with two beaters. As long as the size is suitable, any kitchen container can be used to hold ingredients.

Stand mixer: Larger and more powerful than its handheld equivalent, a stand mixer has a special bowl that locks into place and usually comes with a wire whisk, flat beater, and dough hook for whipping, mixing, and kneading.

Immersion blender: A handheld blender used for puréeing soups, sauces, and other liquids directly in the cooking vessel.

Ready to see everything matzo can do? Let's get started!

My dad, second from left, at the factory circa 1950s.

YENTA   a busybody

BREAKFASTS

CHEESY LEMON PANCAKES . . . 19

MATZO GRANOLA . . . 22

BLUEBERRY AND CHEESE BLINTZES . . . 23

MATZO CHILAQUILES . . . 26

L.E.O. MATZO BREI . . . 29

CHEESY LEMON PANCAKES

1 cup whole milk

3 large eggs, separated

2 tablespoons sugar

Zest and juice of 1 lemon

1 teaspoon kosher salt

1 cup matzo cake meal

¼ cup potato starch

1½ teaspoons baking powder

¾ cup cottage cheese or Homemade Ricotta (page 20)

Unsalted butter, for greasing the pan

Confectioners' sugar, fruit, or maple syrup, for serving (optional)

Lemon and ricotta go together in pancakes like two peas in a pod, but ricotta is difficult to use during Passover, as most brands use a grain-based vinegar in production. For this reason, we developed the recipe using cottage cheese instead, which makes a very tasty and traditional substitute. But we've also included an amazingly simple recipe for homemade, kosher for Passover ricotta cheese that is absolutely worth the effort! If you make the recipe outside the holiday and don't care about the vinegar, store-bought ricotta is just fine.   SERVES 4

1   In a large bowl, whisk together the milk, egg yolks, sugar, lemon zest and juice, and salt. In a medium bowl, sift together the cake meal, potato starch, and baking powder. Add the dry ingredients to the wet, using a rubber spatula to mix until just combined. Take care not to overmix or the pancakes will be tough.

2   Using a stand mixer fitted with the whisk attachment or a whisk and a large bowl, whip the egg whites until soft peaks form. They should look like soft-serve ice cream. Using a rubber spatula, gently fold one-third of the egg whites at a time into the batter until well incorporated, taking care not to overfold. Gently fold in the cheese—the batter should be streaky with visible lumps of cheese curds throughout.

3   Melt 1 to 2 tablespoons butter in a large nonstick skillet over medium heat. Add ¼ cup of the batter for each pancake, working in batches if needed. Cook the pancakes until the edges are golden brown and bubbles begin to form on top, about 5 minutes. Flip and cook until the second side is golden, another 2 minutes. Serve with confectioners' sugar, fresh fruit, maple syrup, or your favorite pancake topper.

HOMEMADE RICOTTA

MAKES 1½ QUARTS

3 quarts whole milk, not ultra-homogenized

1½ cups heavy cream

3 tablespoons kosher salt

½ teaspoon freshly ground black pepper

¼ cup plus 2 tablespoons fresh lemon juice

1 Line a colander with 3 layers of cheesecloth and set over a large bowl. In a large pot over medium-high heat, bring the milk, cream, salt, and pepper to a full, rapid boil.

2 Add the lemon juice, reduce the heat to low, and simmer for 5 minutes. You will see the dairy "break" and curds start to form. Pour the mixture through the cheesecloth and allow to drain for 20 minutes. It should be thick, like cottage cheese.

3 Transfer the cheese to a medium bowl, place plastic wrap directly on the surface, and refrigerate until fully cooled, 30 minutes. Store in an airtight container in the refrigerator for up to 1 week.

Streit's Matzo and Vita Herring—what could be better?

MATZO
GRANOLA

2¾ cups matzo farfel

1 cup unsweetened coconut chips

1 cup shelled raw pistachios

1 cup sliced almonds

½ cup (packed) light brown sugar

⅓ cup maple syrup

⅓ cup extra-virgin olive oil

1 teaspoon ground cinnamon

1 tablespoon kosher salt

⅓ cup golden raisins

⅓ cup dried cherries

This granola is great to make at the beginning of the week and have on hand for a light breakfast or snack. Feel free to use our recipe as a base to create your own, personalized version. As long as the total amounts of nuts and seeds stay the same, the types and ratios can change and the recipe will still work beautifully. **MAKES 6 CUPS**

1 Preheat the oven to 300°F. Line two baking sheets with parchment paper.

2 In a large bowl, toss together all of the ingredients except the raisins and dried cherries. Mix until everything is evenly coated. Spread the mixture over the baking sheets.

3 Transfer to the oven and bake, stirring every 8 to 10 minutes, until the granola is dry and light golden, about 35 minutes. Remove from the oven and stir in the raisins and dried cherries. Allow to cool to room temperature before storing in airtight containers. The granola will stay fresh for about 2 months stored at room temperature.

 CHUTZPAH   nerve or gall

BLUEBERRY AND CHEESE
BLINTZES

CRÊPES

1½ cups whole milk, plus more as needed

⅔ cup matzo meal

2 large eggs

3 tablespoons unsalted butter, melted and cooled slightly, plus more for the skillet

½ teaspoon kosher salt

COMPOTE

1¼ cups fresh blueberries

¼ cup sugar

1 tablespoon fresh lemon juice

¾ teaspoon potato starch

¼ teaspoon kosher salt

FILLING

1¼ cups 4% small-curd cottage cheese

¼ cup sour cream

1 large egg yolk

1 tablespoon sugar

For those who love the comfort of blintzes, here's a way to get your fix—even on Passover mornings. Feel free to experiment with different fruit compotes or other toppings to make the recipe your own. The crêpe batter can be made in advance and refrigerated in an airtight container for up to two days. **SERVES 4 (MAKES 12 BLINTZES)**

1 Combine the crêpe batter ingredients in a blender or food processor, or whisk by hand in a medium bowl until smooth. Place in an airtight container and refrigerate for at least 30 minutes.

2 Meanwhile, in a medium pot over medium-high heat, stir together all of the ingredients for the blueberry compote. Simmer until the berries begin to break down and the juices thicken, about 5 minutes. Pour the compote into a bowl and place in the refrigerator to cool, about 15 minutes.

3 Heat a small nonstick skillet or crêpe pan over medium-high heat. Stir the chilled crêpe batter, adding a tablespoon or two of milk to thin it out until pourable, if needed. Lightly brush the skillet with melted butter and immediately add ¼ cup of the batter, tilting the pan in a circular motion to coat the surface evenly. Cook the crêpe until the bottom begins to brown, about 30 seconds. Using a spatula, loosen the crêpe and flip it over, grabbing the edge with your fingers if necessary. Continue to cook the crêpe on the second side until it's just set and lightly browned, another 20 seconds, then slide it onto a plate. Repeat the process with the remaining batter, stacking the finished crêpes one on top of another (don't worry, they won't stick together!). Use them right away or refrigerate

recipe continues

them, wrapped in plastic, for up to 2 days. The crêpes also freeze well if layered with parchment paper, then covered with plastic wrap.

4 Preheat the oven to 400°F. Line a baking sheet with aluminum foil.

5 In a medium bowl, mix the cottage cheese, sour cream, egg yolk, and sugar. Set the top crêpe from the stack on your work surface. Place 3 tablespoons of the cheese filling and 1 tablespoon of the blueberry compote in the center of the bottom third of the crêpe, leaving a ¾-inch border around the lower edge. Fold the sides over the filling and roll the crêpe from the bottom up, like

you would wrap a burrito. Place seam side down on the prepared baking sheet and repeat with the remaining crêpes, cheese filling, and blueberry compote. You should have about 1 cup of compote left over.

6 Place a large skillet over medium-high heat and brush with melted butter. Heat until the butter just begins to smoke, then add the blintzes and panfry until golden brown, 2 minutes per side. Transfer back to the prepared sheet and place in the oven until warmed through, about 10 minutes. Serve with the remaining blueberry compote or your favorite topping.

Turning the matzo to prevent burning.

MATZO
CHILAQUILES

SALSA VERDE

2 pounds tomatillos, husked and diced

2 white onions, diced (2 cups)

3 garlic cloves

1 jalapeño pepper, halved lengthwise (remove seeds if less heat is desired)

2 tablespoons extra-virgin olive oil

½ teaspoon chili powder

½ cup fresh cilantro leaves

Kosher salt and freshly ground pepper

Neutral oil, for frying

5 sheets of matzo, broken into 2-inch pieces

1 red onion, thinly sliced (about 1 cup)

1½ cups crumbled feta or queso fresco

¼ cup chopped fresh cilantro

8 large eggs (optional)

Sour cream (optional)

Can you say breakfast for dinner? This new twist on a classic Mexican dish is so worth the effort. Deep-frying matzo completely transforms it. Slowly simmered in a fresh, homemade salsa verde and topped with a couple of eggs prepared your favorite way, this dish is sure to make you *kvell*. SERVES 4

1 Preheat the oven to 450°F.

2 For the salsa verde, combine the tomatillos, onion, garlic, jalapeño, olive oil, and chili powder in a large roasting pan. Roast for 30 minutes, until the tomatillos begin to char and soften. Transfer the cooked vegetables to a food processor, add the cilantro, and blend until smooth. Season to taste with salt and pepper and set aside.

3 Meanwhile, pour 2 inches of oil into a large pot fitted with a deep-fry thermometer and heat over medium-high heat to 350°F. Working in batches, fry the matzo until evenly golden brown, about 1 minute. Drain on paper towels and season with salt.

4 In a large skillet over medium heat, bring the salsa verde to a simmer. Add the fried matzo and cook until just softened but not soggy, about 2 minutes. Divide the chilaquiles among 4 plates, topping with sliced onion, crumbled cheese, and cilantro. If desired, top each serving with 2 eggs prepared in your favorite way and a dollop of sour cream to cut the heat.

TIP If you don't have a deep-fry thermometer, you can still check the oil temperature using the wooden spoon method. Dip the handle of a wooden spoon (or a chopstick) into the oil and watch what happens. If it starts to bubble steadily, the oil is hot enough for frying. If it bubbles vigorously, the oil is too hot and needs to cool off a touch. If none or very few bubbles pop up, it's not yet hot enough.

KVELL beam with pride, be delighted with

L.E.O. MATZO
BREI

4 sheets of matzo

3 tablespoons unsalted butter

1 large sweet onion, halved and thinly sliced (about 1 cup)

8 large eggs

1 teaspoon kosher salt and ¼ teaspoon freshly ground black pepper

4 ounces lox or smoked salmon, cut into ½-inch-wide strips

1 tablespoon chopped fresh dill

1 tablespoon chopped fresh chives

1½ tablespoons drained capers

Lox, eggs, and onions, or L.E.O., as the combination is commonly known, is as quintessential to Jewish food as the bagel. Right after I learned to talk, I'm sure the next thing my father taught me to do was eat L.E.O. We took this classic and married it with matzo brei to make these two iconic dishes even more beloved. My dad would be proud! SERVES 4

1 Run each sheet of matzo under cold running water for 15 seconds until it just begins to soften but isn't falling apart. Break into 1½-inch pieces and set aside.

2 Melt 1 tablespoon of the butter in a large nonstick skillet over medium-high heat. Add the onion slices in a single layer and cook without stirring until they turn dark brown in spots, 3 minutes. Reduce the heat to medium, add the remaining butter, stir the onions, and continue to cook until they are evenly golden brown, 4 minutes.

3 Meanwhile, beat the eggs in a medium bowl. Season with the salt and black pepper. Stir in the matzo and let soak for 1 minute.

4 Reduce the heat under the skillet to medium-low. Add the egg-matzo mixture and gently stir as though you were making scrambled eggs. Once the eggs begin to set, about 3 minutes, add the lox, dill, chives, and capers. Continue to stir until the eggs are cooked through but still soft, about 1 minute, or to desired consistency.

VERKLEMPT choked up, emotional, on the verge of tears

STARTERS

CLASSIC CHICKEN SOUP WITH MATZO BALLS . . . 32

CHICKEN-STUFFED WHOLE-WHEAT
MATZO BALLS IN THYME-MUSHROOM BROTH . . . 35

PAPA POMODORO
(TUSCAN TOMATO MATZO SOUP) . . . 38

CAESAR SALAD WITH SMOKED WHITEFISH
AND MATZO BALL CROUTONS . . . 41

GREEK MATZO PANZANELLA . . . 42

EASY CHOPPED LIVER WITH PICKLED ONIONS. . . 44

CLASSIC CHICKEN SOUP

MATZO BALLS

STOCK

4 pounds chicken wings

2 pounds chicken breasts, on the rib

2 yellow onions, diced (2 cups)

2 carrots, diced (1 cup)

2 celery stalks, diced (½ cup)

8 garlic cloves

2 bay leaves

4 sprigs of fresh thyme

MATZO BALLS

4 large eggs

¼ cup seltzer

¼ cup schmaltz (see Tip) or vegetable oil

1 cup matzo meal

¼ teaspoon baking powder

1 teaspoon kosher salt

⅛ teaspoon freshly ground black pepper

Kosher salt to taste

2 tablespoons chopped fresh dill

3 carrots, diced (1 cup)

Better known as "Jewish penicillin," matzo ball soup is a staple all year round. Some insist the matzo ball must be light as air, while others prefer a denser ball that sits on the bottom of the bowl. After many "sinker versus floater" trials, we can confidently say these matzo balls are the best of both worlds.   SERVES 6 TO 8 (MAKES 24 BALLS)

1 Combine 4 quarts water and all the stock ingredients in a 5- to 6-quart stockpot over high heat. Bring to a boil, then reduce the heat to medium-low and simmer for 2 hours, periodically skimming and discarding any foam or fat that rises to the top.

2 Meanwhile, in a large bowl, combine the eggs, seltzer, and schmaltz. In a small bowl, mix the matzo meal, baking powder, salt, and pepper. Add the dry ingredients to the wet and stir to combine. Place in the refrigerator, uncovered, to chill for 30 minutes.

3 When the stock is finished, strain it through a fine-mesh sieve, discarding the vegetables and setting aside the chicken meat until it is cool enough to handle, about 10 minutes. Reserve 2 cups of chicken for the finished soup; the rest makes great chicken salad or can be used in another recipe. You should have about 4 quarts of stock.

4 Season the stock with salt, pour 2 quarts back into the large pot, and bring to a simmer over low heat. Place the remaining 2 quarts in a small pot with the dill, diced carrots, and the 2 cups reserved chicken meat, and set aside.

recipe continues

TIP To make your own schmaltz, slowly simmer 1 pound of chicken skin and fat trimmings with 2 tablespoons water in a small pot over low heat for 1 to 2 hours, stirring occasionally. Once the skin has browned and crisped, strain the schmaltz and store in the refrigerator.

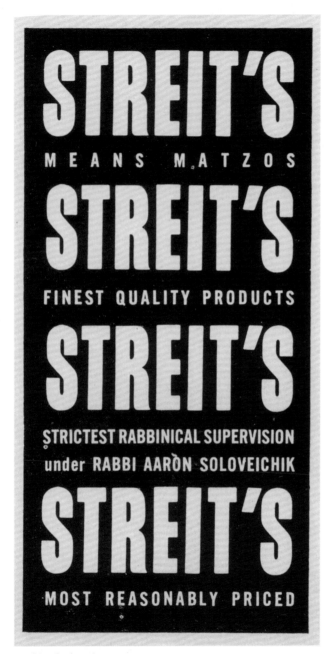

Archived advertisement.

5 With wet hands, form the chilled matzo mixture into 1½-inch balls. Add to the large pot of simmering stock. Cover and cook over medium-low heat until the matzo balls are cooked through and at least doubled in size, 1 hour. Meanwhile, simmer the small pot of soup until the carrots are just cooked through, 5 to 7 minutes.

6 Using a slotted spoon, transfer the matzo balls to soup bowls and ladle over the soup with the dill, carrots, and chicken. The cloudy matzo ball cooking liquid may be saved for another use.

CHICKEN-STUFFED WHOLE-WHEAT MATZO BALLS
IN THYME-MUSHROOM BROTH

BROTH

2 tablespoons olive oil

2 yellow onions, diced (2 cups)

1 carrot, diced (½ cup)

4 garlic cloves, chopped

Kosher salt

3 pounds white button mushrooms, sliced, plus 6 mushrooms, thinly sliced

8 fresh flat-leaf parsley stems

8 sprigs of fresh thyme, plus 2 tablespoons fresh thyme leaves

2 bay leaves

2 teaspoons black peppercorns

MEATBALLS

2 tablespoons schmaltz (see Tip on page 32) or vegetable oil

1 yellow onion, finely chopped (1 cup)

2 tablespoons fresh thyme leaves

3½ ounces shiitake mushrooms, finely chopped (1 cup)

Kosher salt and freshly ground black pepper

1 pound ground chicken, preferably dark meat

3 large eggs

⅓ cup matzo meal, plus more if needed

It's hard to reinvent something as iconic as Grandma's *knaidlach* (that's Yiddish for matzo balls), but by stuffing them with shiitake-chicken meatballs, we believe we have succeeded. The textural contrast of the earthy meatball surrounded by the airy layer of matzo ball makes this a perfect dish when warming up for Passover.

SERVES 6 TO 8 (MAKES 24 BALLS)

1 For the mushroom broth, heat the oil in a 6- to 8-quart stockpot over medium heat. When it begins to shimmer, add the onion, carrot, and garlic. Season with salt and cook, stirring often, until soft and translucent, 3 minutes. Increase the heat to medium-high and add the 3 pounds of mushrooms, the parsley stems, thyme sprigs, bay leaves, and peppercorns. Cook, stirring occasionally, until the mushrooms have softened and released their liquid, 6 minutes. Add 5 quarts water and bring to a boil, then reduce the heat to medium-low and simmer the stock until it has developed a strong mushroom flavor, about 1 hour.

2 Meanwhile, for the meatballs, heat the schmaltz in a medium skillet over medium heat. When it begins to shimmer, add the onion and cook, stirring frequently, until caramelized, about 20 minutes. If the onion starts to burn, reduce the heat and add a tablespoon of water at a time. Add the thyme and cook until aromatic, another 30 seconds. Increase the heat to medium-high and add the shiitakes to the skillet. Cook, stirring often, until softened and starting to brown, 4 minutes. Season with salt and pepper. Remove from the pan and set aside on a plate to cool.

recipe continues

MATZO BALLS

6 large eggs

¼ cup plus 2 tablespoons seltzer

¼ cup plus 2 tablespoons schmaltz (see Tip on page 32) or vegetable oil

1½ cups whole-wheat matzo meal

⅜ teaspoon baking powder

1½ teaspoons salt

¼ teaspoon freshly ground black pepper

3 Make the matzo balls: In a large bowl, combine the eggs, seltzer, and schmaltz. In a small bowl, mix the matzo meal, baking powder, salt, and pepper. Add the dry ingredients to the wet and stir to combine. Place in the refrigerator, uncovered, to chill for 30 minutes.

4 To finish the meatballs, in a medium bowl, combine the chicken, eggs, matzo meal, and reserved mushroom mixture. Taking care not to overmix, add more matzo meal as needed to be able to shape the meatballs. With wet hands, form the mixture into 1¼-inch balls and set aside on a plate or baking sheet.

5 With wet hands, pinch off a golf ball–sized portion of matzo ball dough. Flatten it between your palms, place an uncooked meatball in the center, and pinch the edges together to fully cover the meatball. Roll the filled matzo ball in your hands to smooth it out, pinching together any holes. Repeat with the remaining filling and matzo balls.

6 When the stock is finished, strain it through a fine-mesh sieve, discarding the vegetables. You should have about 4 quarts of finished stock. Season the stock with salt, pour 2 quarts back into the large pot, and bring to a simmer over medium-low heat. Place the other 2 quarts in a medium pot and set aside. Add the matzo balls to the large pot, cover, and simmer until cooked through, 1 hour.

7 When the matzo balls are done, add the thinly sliced mushrooms and the thyme leaves to the reserved 2 quarts of stock and heat over medium-low heat.

8 Using a slotted spoon, transfer the stuffed matzo balls to the serving bowls. Ladle over the clear mushroom soup and serve. The cloudy matzo ball cooking liquid can be saved for another use.

 BUPKIS nothing

PAPA POMODORO
(TUSCAN TOMATO MATZO SOUP)

PARVE
(DAIRY WITH
CHEESE GARNISH)

3 tablespoons extra-virgin olive oil,
plus more for drizzling

½ yellow onion, diced (about ½ cup)

½ fennel bulb, diced (about ½ cup)

2 garlic cloves, thinly sliced

Kosher salt and freshly ground
black pepper

¼ teaspoon dried red pepper flakes

1 28-ounce can whole, peeled
tomatoes, crushed by hand, or 2
pounds fresh tomatoes, blanched,
peeled, and chopped

2 cups vegetable stock

2 sprigs of fresh basil, plus 3
tablespoons chopped, for garnish

3 sheets of matzo, broken into small
pieces (or 1½ cups matzo farfel)

¼ cup grated Parmesan cheese
(optional)

This recipe is all about the tomatoes, so use the best ones you can find. During the summer and fall, blanching and peeling ripe fresh tomatoes delivers a soup that tastes like it came right from the garden. During the colder months, when they are out of season in most places, we look to high-quality canned tomatoes. Not only does the matzo thicken the soup, but it also adds a wonderfully nutty flavor. **SERVES 4 TO 6**

1 Heat the olive oil in a large pot over medium heat. When it begins to shimmer, add the onion, fennel, and garlic, season with ¼ teaspoon salt, and cook, stirring often, until soft and translucent, 10 minutes.

2 Sprinkle the red pepper flakes into the pot and cook for 30 seconds, then add the crushed tomatoes, vegetable stock, and basil sprigs. Season with salt and black pepper. Increase the heat to medium-high and bring the soup to a boil; then reduce the heat to low. When it begins to simmer, add the matzo and cook, stirring occasionally, until the soup has thickened to a porridge-like consistency, 30 minutes.

3 Remove the basil and, using an immersion blender (or a food processor), blend the soup until smooth. Season with salt and pepper to taste. Serve in warm bowls, garnished with a drizzle of olive oil, the chopped basil, and Parmesan cheese, if desired.

TIP Traditionally, this soup is thick, almost like a sauce. Feel free to add more vegetable stock to adjust to your desired consistency.

 UNGAPACHKA everything but the kitchen sink

CAESAR SALAD
WITH SMOKED WHITEFISH
AND MATZO BALL CROUTONS

MATZO BALL CROUTONS

4 tablespoons extra-virgin olive oil

½ teaspoon garlic powder

½ teaspoon dried oregano

7 cooked 2½-inch matzo balls, store-bought or homemade (page 32), chilled, dried, and quartered

Kosher salt and freshly ground black pepper

CAESAR DRESSING

½ garlic clove

⅛ teaspoon kosher salt

2 tablespoons fresh lemon juice (from about 1 lemon)

1 tablespoon mayonnaise

1 teaspoon Dijon mustard

¾ teaspoon anchovy paste

¼ teaspoon freshly ground black pepper

4 teaspoons extra-virgin olive oil

8 cups romaine lettuce, washed, dried, and torn

18 ounces smoked whitefish, skinned, boned, and coarsely flaked

This hearty salad is a fun way to use leftover matzo balls. (How many times can you eat soup, after all?) Leave the matzo balls unwrapped overnight in the fridge on paper towels the day before you want to make these croutons. Be sure to serve them just a few minutes after they come out of the oven, while they are still crispy and warm. The Caesar dressing here is dairy free to make this salad kosher for Passover, but feel free to include a sprinkle of Parmesan cheese if you do not keep a kosher diet. **SERVES 4**

1 Make the croutons: Preheat the oven to 325°F. In a medium bowl, whisk together 2 tablespoons of the olive oil, the garlic powder, and oregano. Add the matzo balls, season with salt and pepper, and gently toss to coat.

2 Line a baking sheet with aluminum foil and coat with the remaining 2 tablespoons olive oil. Spread the seasoned matzo balls on the baking sheet, transfer to the oven, and bake, tossing every 20 minutes, until golden brown and crispy, about 1½ hours. Remove from the oven and allow to cool for 15 minutes before serving.

3 Meanwhile, make the dressing: In a small bowl, use a fork to mash the garlic and salt into a paste. Add the mayonnaise, mustard, anchovy paste, and black pepper. Whisk until smooth. Still whisking, slowly drizzle in the oil until emulsified.

4 In a large bowl, toss the lettuce, whitefish, croutons, and dressing together until everything is evenly coated. Divide among salad plates and serve.

TIP Prefer a *schmear*? Whitefish salad is a great substitute for the smoked whitefish.

GREEK MATZO
PANZANELLA

1 red onion, thinly sliced (1 cup)

2 tablespoons extra-virgin olive oil

6 sheets of matzo

Kosher salt and freshly ground
   black pepper

VINAIGRETTE

1 garlic clove, minced

½ teaspoon Dijon mustard

2 teaspoons dried oregano

2 tablespoons fresh lemon juice
   (from about 1 lemon)

½ teaspoon honey

¼ cup red wine vinegar

½ cup extra-virgin olive oil

Kosher salt and freshly ground
   black pepper

2 cups watercress, large stems
   removed

1 pint cherry tomatoes, halved
   (2 cups)

1 cucumber, halved lengthwise,
   seeded, and cut into ¼-inch slices

1 cup crumbled feta

1 cup black olives, pitted

This traditionally Tuscan salad was created as a way to use up day-old bread, featuring it alongside lots of fresh veggies. Here, we give it a Mediterranean spin and swap in matzo for the *hametz*, of course. Tasty and super easy. What's not to love? SERVES 4

1 Preheat the oven to 400°F. Line a baking sheet with aluminum foil.

2 Place the red onion and a few ice cubes in a small bowl and cover with cold water. Let sit for about 15 minutes, then drain, rinse, and pat dry.

3 Meanwhile, brush olive oil on both sides of the matzos and season with salt and pepper. Lay them out on the prepared baking sheet and transfer to the oven to toast until lightly browned, 5 to 6 minutes. Remove from the oven, allow to cool for 5 minutes, then roughly break into 1½-inch squares and set aside.

4 Make the dressing: In a small bowl, whisk together the garlic, mustard, oregano, lemon juice, honey, and vinegar. Whisking constantly, slowly stream in the olive oil until emulsified. Season with salt and pepper.

5 In a large bowl, combine the watercress, tomatoes, cucumbers, feta, olives, red onion, and matzo. Season with salt and pepper. Pour the dressing over the salad and gently toss to combine, taking care not to break up the matzo further. Allow the salad to sit for 10 minutes so the matzo can soften and absorb the dressing. Divide among salad plates and serve.

TIP Soaking the red onion slices in ice water not only eliminates their strong raw flavor, but also makes them extra crunchy.

EASY CHOPPED LIVER
WITH PICKLED ONIONS

1 pound fresh chicken livers

Kosher salt and freshly ground
   black pepper

½ cup schmaltz (see Tip on page 32)
   or extra-virgin olive oil

3 yellow onions, diced (3 cups)

2 bay leaves

2 hard-boiled eggs, chopped

½ teaspoon balsamic vinegar

5 sheets of matzo

2 tablespoons extra-virgin olive oil

1 tablespoon fresh thyme leaves

Pickled Onions (recipe follows)

This recipe is for all those people who remember their bubbies grinding chicken livers in a meat grinder—the kind that screwed onto a table. What *tsuris*! Our alternative takes half the time! Just be sure to chill the chopped liver for at least two hours before serving. When stored in an airtight container, it will hold in the refrigerator for up to one week. **MAKES 8 APPETIZER SERVINGS**

1 Preheat the oven to 400°F. Line a baking sheet with aluminum foil.

2 Pat the chicken livers dry and season liberally with salt and pepper. Heat 2 tablespoons of the schmaltz in a large skillet over medium-high heat. When it begins to shimmer, add a few livers, working in batches if needed, and sauté until lightly browned on the outside but still pink in the middle, about 2 minutes per side. Transfer to a plate with a slotted spoon and set aside to cool.

3 Reduce the heat to low. Add the remaining schmaltz and the onion and bay leaves to the skillet. Season with salt and pepper, and cook, stirring often, until the onions are caramelized, about 30 minutes. Remove the onions and any remaining schmaltz from the skillet, discard the bay leaves, and allow to cool to room temperature.

4 Transfer the chicken livers to a food processor and pulse until you reach the desired consistency. Alternatively, roughly chop them until they are smooth with a few chunky pieces remaining. Place the livers in a large bowl, add the onion-schmaltz mixture, eggs, and balsamic vinegar. Mix well and season with salt and pepper to taste.

5 Brush the matzos on both sides with olive oil and sprinkle with thyme, salt, and pepper. Lay them out on the prepared baking sheet and place in the oven to toast until lightly browned, 5 to 6 minutes. Remove the matzos and allow to cool, then break into 2-inch square crackers. Serve on a platter alongside a bowl of the chopped liver topped with drained pickled onions.

TSURIS trouble, distress, problem

PICKLED ONIONS

MAKES 4 CUPS

1 cup white wine or champagne
vinegar

2 tablespoons sugar

½ tablespoon kosher salt

2 red onions, halved and thinly
sliced

In a small pot over high heat, combine 1 cup water, the vinegar, sugar, and salt and bring to a boil. Place the onions in a medium heatproof bowl and pour the boiling pickling liquid over them. Set aside to cool to room temperature. Refrigerate in an airtight container, submerged in their liquid. They are best served cold and will keep for about 3 months.

TIP Stuck with leftover pickling juice? It can be used as a seasoned vinegar to make salad dressings, amp up braised chicken, season potato salad, or make yogurt into a simple dip. You can also bring it back to a boil, add more sugar and salt, and pour it over more onions to make a second batch.

Forgot to get a salami for your guy in the army?
No problem—egg matzos for all!

SIDES AND SNACKS

MATZO NACHOS
WITH PICKLED JALAPEÑOS . . . 49

POTATO, BROCCOLI, AND MATZO GRATIN . . . 53

ZUCCHINI LATKES WITH DILL YOGURT . . . 54

MOROCCAN MATZO STUFFING . . . 57

PEAR AND CHERRY MATZO KUGEL . . . 59

SAVORY AND SWEET TOASTS . . . 64

MATZO NACHOS
WITH PICKLED JALAPEÑOS

4 plum tomatoes, diced (1 cup)

½ white onion, diced (½ cup)

1 jalapeño pepper, seeds removed, diced

2 tablespoons fresh lime juice (from about 1 lime)

¼ cup chopped fresh cilantro, plus whole cilantro leaves for garnish

1 tablespoon extra-virgin olive oil

Kosher salt and freshly ground black pepper

Neutral oil, for frying

5 sheets of matzo, broken into 2-inch pieces

1 cup grated Cheddar or Mexican-style cheese blend

About 1 cup Pickled Jalapeños (page 50)

1 avocado, diced

½ cup sour cream or Greek yogurt

We've fallen hard for deep-fried matzo, and you will, too. Turning crunchy, crispy matzo into nachos just makes sense—and these toppings really take this recipe to the next level. The pickled jalapeño recipe makes more than needed for the nachos, but they are a staple to keep on hand in the refrigerator—terrific on sandwiches for a hit of flavor and spice.   SERVES 4

1 In a small bowl, stir together the tomatoes, onion, jalapeño, lime juice, cilantro, and olive oil. Season with salt and pepper. Set the salsa aside.

2 Preheat the oven to 400°F. Prepare 2 baking sheets, one lined with paper towels and the other with aluminum foil.

3 Pour at least 2 inches of a neutral oil into a large pot fitted with a deep-fry thermometer. (If you don't have a thermometer, see the wooden spoon method on page 26.) Heat to 350°F over medium-high heat. Working in batches, add the matzo pieces and fry until evenly golden brown, about 1 minute. Place on the paper towel–lined baking sheet to drain and season with salt.

4 Transfer the fried matzo to the foil-lined baking sheet and cover with the grated cheese. Bake until the cheese melts, 5 minutes.

5 Transfer the nachos to a large platter and top with the tomato salsa, pickled jalapeños, avocado, cilantro leaves, and sour cream. Serve.

TIP For a lighter twist on a classic pairing, substitute Greek yogurt for sour cream.

PICKLED JALAPEÑOS

MAKES ABOUT 2 CUPS

1 cup white wine vinegar or
    champagne vinegar

2 tablespoons sugar

1½ teaspoons kosher salt

8 jalapeños, sliced into ¼-inch-thick
    rounds

Combine the vinegar, sugar, salt, and 1 cup water in a small saucepan over high heat and bring to a boil. Place the jalapeños in a heatproof bowl and pour the boiling pickling liquid over them. Set aside to cool to room temperature. Store the jalapeños in an airtight container, submerged in the liquid, in the refrigerator. Once fully chilled, they are ready to eat, and will last for months in the refrigerator.

SCHVITZ   sweat, perspire

Streit's advertising circa 1940s.

POTATO, BROCCOLI, AND
MATZO GRATIN

2 tablespoons extra-virgin olive oil, plus more for greasing the dish

1 cup heavy cream

1¾ cups whole milk

1 tablespoon potato starch

1 pound russet potatoes, peeled and sliced paper-thin (see Tip)

2 cups shredded Cheddar cheese

4 cups small broccoli florets (about 1 large head)

2 cups matzo farfel

Kosher salt and freshly ground black pepper

Using matzo farfel, we have combined two of our favorite side dishes, potato gratin and broccoli with Cheddar cheese. It makes for a substantial side dish that goes great with a dairy dinner.   **SERVES 4 TO 6**

1 Preheat the oven to 400°F. Grease a 9-inch square baking dish.

2 In a large bowl, whisk together the cream, milk, and potato starch until the starch dissolves. Add the potatoes and toss to coat. In a separate large bowl, toss together 1 cup of the Cheddar, the broccoli, farfel, and the olive oil. Season generously with salt and pepper.

3 Pick out half of the potato slices from the cream mixture and lay them in the prepared baking dish, covering the bottom completely. Top with the Cheddar, broccoli, and farfel mixture. Spoon half the cream mixture over the filling to just cover it.

4 Lay the remaining potato slices over the filling so that it is completely covered. Pour the remaining cream mixture over the top and sprinkle with the remaining cheese.

5 Cover the baking dish with aluminum foil and bake for 20 minutes. Remove the foil and continue cooking until the cream is fully absorbed by the potatoes and the cheese is golden brown, about 45 minutes more. Allow the gratin to sit for 15 minutes before cutting and serving.

KVETCH complain, nag

TIP Using a mandoline or a food processor with a slicing attachment is the best and easiest way to get perfectly uniform, thin slices of potato. But a sharp knife works just fine, too!

ZUCCHINI LATKES
~WITH~ DILL YOGURT

PARVE
(DAIRY WHEN SERVED
WITH YOGURT)

2 large zucchini, yellow squash, or a combination, grated (2 cups)

Kosher salt and freshly ground black pepper

½ small yellow onion, grated (¼ cup)

1 jalapeño pepper, seeds removed, finely chopped

1 large egg, beaten

½ cup matzo meal

3 tablespoons matzo cake meal

1 teaspoon baking powder

Neutral oil, for frying

Dill Yogurt (optional; page 56)

Lemon wedges (optional)

~FUTZ~ to fart around

It seems that every cuisine has a variation on the fried potato pancake. The Swiss have their *rösti*; the Russians make *draniki*; and the Jews enjoy latkes. It's simply one of the most satisfying foods there is: crispy, slightly greasy, and salty. This zucchini alternative is a lighter version that's just as tasty. These golden brown cakes are great when fresh, but they can also be stored in the refrigerator for a few days and reheated until crispy. **SERVES 4 (MAKES ABOUT 12 LATKES)**

1 Toss the squash with 1 teaspoon salt and place in a colander set in the sink to drain for 30 minutes. Transfer to paper towels or a clean kitchen towel and squeeze out any remaining excess liquid. Place in a medium bowl along with the onion, jalapeño, egg, matzo meal, cake meal, and baking powder. Season with salt and pepper. Combine thoroughly and let sit for 5 minutes at room temperature.

2 Preheat the oven to 300°F. Set up two baking sheets: one lined with paper towels and the other with a wire rack.

3 Pour neutral oil into a large skillet to just cover the bottom and heat over medium-high heat. When

it shimmers, spoon in about 1½ tablespoons of the squash batter and gently press down with a spoon so that the latke is about ½ inch thick. Repeat with the remaining batter, working in batches as needed, and cook the latkes until crispy and golden brown, 2 to 3 minutes per side. Set the finished latkes on the paper towel–lined baking sheet to drain, and then transfer them to the wire rack to cool.

4 Once all the latkes are finished, reheat them in the oven, still on the wire rack, for 3 to 5 minutes. Serve with the dill yogurt and lemon wedges, if using.

DILL YOGURT

MAKES 1 CUP

1 cup Greek yogurt

3 tablespoons chopped fresh dill

¼ teaspoon chili powder

Juice and grated zest of ½ lemon

¼ teaspoon kosher salt

In a small bowl, mix all the ingredients. Place in an airtight container and refrigerate for up to 1 week.

The beginning of our business on the Lower East Side—Rivington Street.

MOROCCAN MATZO
STUFFING

4 ounces pistachios, coarsely chopped (1 cup)

7 cups matzo farfel

2 tablespoons extra-virgin olive oil, plus more for greasing the dish

2 yellow onions, diced (2 cups)

3 celery stalks, diced (1 cup)

2 carrots, diced (1 cup)

½ teaspoon ground cinnamon

½ teaspoon ground cumin

¼ teaspoon dried red pepper flakes

¼ cup chopped fresh flat-leaf parsley

½ cup golden raisins

2 cups chicken stock, store-bought or homemade (page 32)

1 large egg, beaten

1 teaspoon grated orange zest

1 tablespoon kosher salt

½ teaspoon freshly ground black pepper

The cuisine of the Sephardic Jews incorporates exotic flavors from the Middle East and Northern Africa. The aromas from cumin, pistachio, cinnamon, orange, and toasted farfel were our inspiration in creating this dish, which will surprise and delight your guests. **SERVES 4 TO 6**

1   Preheat the oven to 400°F. Lightly grease a 9 x 13-inch baking dish.

2   On separate baking sheets, spread out the pistachios and farfel. Transfer both to the oven and toast until light golden brown, about 3 minutes for the pistachios and 5 minutes for the farfel. Remove and set both aside to cool.

3   Meanwhile, heat the olive oil in a large skillet over medium-high heat. When it begins to shimmer, add the onion, celery, and carrots and sauté until the vegetables soften and are lightly caramelized, 8 minutes. Add the cinnamon, cumin, and red pepper flakes and continue to cook until fragrant,

30 seconds. Transfer the mixture to a large bowl and let cool to room temperature, about 10 minutes.

4   Add the farfel, pistachios, parsley, raisins, chicken stock, egg, orange zest, salt, and pepper to the vegetables. Mix thoroughly to combine. Spoon the stuffing into the prepared baking dish, but don't pack it too tightly—the looser the stuffing, the crispier it will get while cooking. Cover the dish with aluminum foil and bake for 30 minutes. Remove the foil and continue to bake until the stuffing is golden brown and the top is nicely crisped, 15 minutes more. Remove and let sit for 10 minutes before serving.

PEAR AND CHERRY
MATZO KUGEL

PARVE
(DAIRY IF YOU
USE BUTTER
AND ICE CREAM)

4 Anjou pears, cored and diced

½ cup (packed) light brown sugar

¼ cup freshly squeezed orange juice

8 large eggs, beaten

2 cups dried cherries

1 teaspoon kosher salt

1 teaspoon ground cinnamon

1½ cups sugar

8 tablespoons (1 stick) margarine or butter, melted, plus more for greasing the dish

6 sheets of matzo, broken into large pieces

4 tablespoons (½ stick) cold margarine or butter, cut into small pieces, for topping the kugel

Grab the ripest pears you can find. The winter fruit and matzo combine to make this the perfect side dish or even dessert—just add vanilla ice cream! It will put a smile on everyone's *punim*. SERVES 12

1 Place a rack in the middle of the oven and preheat the oven to 350°F. Grease a 10 × 14-inch baking dish.

2 In a medium bowl, toss together the pears, brown sugar, and orange juice. In a large bowl, whisk together the eggs, cherries, salt, cinnamon, sugar, and melted margarine.

3 Soak the matzo in warm water until just softened, about 45 seconds. Using your hands, squeeze well to remove excess liquid and add to the egg mixture. Add the pear mixture. Mix well and pour into the prepared dish.

4 Dot the pieces of cold margarine across the top of the kugel. Bake for 1 hour, until the top is golden brown and the kugel is set. If the top browns too quickly, cover with foil. Remove and let sit for 15 minutes before cutting and serving.

TIP Here's another serving option: Instead of using a baking dish, spoon the kugel into a muffin tin to bake as individual portions. The cooking time will reduce to about 20 minutes. Look for the tops of the finished kugels to be golden brown and the centers to be firm and piping-hot.

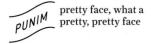 PUNIM pretty face, what a pretty, pretty face

1. WHIPPED CREAM CHEESE, CUCUMBER, RADISH, AND WATERCRESS

2. CRISPY SALAMI AND SCRAMBLED EGGS

3. AVOCADO AND SLOW-ROASTED TOMATO

SAVORY TOASTS

4. CHARRED SCALLION DIP

5. LOX, LEMON YOGURT,
CAPERS, AND DILL

(recipes follow on page 64)

SWEET TOASTS

1. MEXICAN CHOCOLATE GANACHE

2. ICE CREAM SANDWICH WITH CHOCOLATE MATZO

3. MATZO S'MORES

4. PEANUT BUTTER CUP

5. SALTED CARAMEL

(recipes follow on page 64)

SAVORY

1. WHIPPED CREAM CHEESE, CUCUMBER, RADISH, AND WATERCRESS

Spread a sheet of matzo with whipped cream cheese and arrange thin slices of cucumber, radish, and watercress on top. Drizzle with extra-virgin olive oil and fresh lemon juice, then sprinkle with kosher salt and freshly ground black pepper.

2. CRISPY SALAMI AND SCRAMBLED EGGS

Thinly slice some salami and cook in neutral oil until crispy. Scramble some eggs in the same pan. Place the eggs on matzo sheets and top with the crispy salami and some chopped chives.

3. AVOCADO AND SLOW-ROASTED TOMATO

Toss halved cherry tomatoes with kosher salt, extra-virgin olive oil, and a pinch of sugar. Arrange cut side up on a baking sheet and roast for 2½ hours at 250°F. (They will keep for weeks in the refrigerator, covered in olive oil.) Smash some avocado on a slice of matzo, drizzle with olive oil, sprinkle with sea salt, and top with these little tomato flavor bombs.

4. CHARRED SCALLION DIP

Toss 1 bunch of trimmed scallions with neutral oil and lay on a baking sheet. Broil until completely blackened, about 10 minutes. Using a food processor or blender, combine a little of the scallions at a time into a pint of sour cream, tasting as you go to make sure the dip does not become bitter. Season with kosher salt, freshly ground black pepper, and 1 tablespoon of fresh lemon juice. Smear over pieces of matzo that have been brushed with olive oil, sprinkled with salt, and toasted. You'll never reach for an onion soup packet again.

5. LOX, LEMON YOGURT, CAPERS, AND DILL

Mix 1 cup yogurt with the grated zest of 1 lemon, 1 tablespoon fresh lemon juice, 1 tablespoon extra-virgin olive oil, and a pinch of kosher salt. Spread over sheets of matzo, sprinkle with some capers, lay on slices of lox, and top with chopped fresh dill. A few slices of pickled red onion (page 45) are the perfect finishing touch.

SWEET

1. MEXICAN CHOCOLATE GANACHE

In a medium bowl, combine 8 ounces dark chocolate chips (or chopped chocolate), ½ teaspoon ground cinnamon, 1 teaspoon chili powder, ½ teaspoon cayenne, and ½ teaspoon vanilla extract. Bring ½ cup heavy cream just to a boil, then pour it into the bowl. Whisk until smooth and melted. Enjoy spread across matzo, either warm or chilled, for a spicy treat.

2. ICE CREAM SANDWICH WITH CHOCOLATE MATZO

Melt some chocolate either in the microwave or in a small bowl over simmering water. Dip an even number of 4-inch matzo squares in the chocolate to fully coat. Set on a lightly greased baking sheet and chill in the freezer until firm, 10 to 15 minutes. Scoop your favorite ice cream onto a piece of matzo, top with another piece, and gently squeeze them together to spread out the ice cream. Wrap in plastic and return to the freezer to solidify for about 1 hour.

3. MATZO S'MORES

Lay an even number of 4-inch squares of matzo on a baking sheet and toast them under the broiler until light golden brown. Top half the squares with marshmallows; set the remainder aside. Return the baking sheet to the broiler until the marshmallows are toasted, then top each marshmallow with a piece of chocolate and a square of the remaining toasted matzo.

4. PEANUT BUTTER CUP

Melt some chocolate either in the microwave or in a small bowl over simmering water. Spread two 3-inch square matzo pieces with a thin layer of peanut butter and dip into the chocolate to cover completely. Sprinkle with sea salt and place in the freezer to firm up for 10 to 15 minutes. Store in an airtight container or zip-top bag at room temperature or in the refrigerator, if you prefer the peanut butter cups cold.

5. SALTED CARAMEL

In a medium pot, cook 1 cup sugar over medium heat until melted and deep amber in color. Swirl the pan as the sugar starts to darken to keep it cooking evenly. Add 6 tablespoons unsalted butter; it will bubble up aggressively, but whisk until melted. Add ½ cup heavy cream and 1 teaspoon sea salt, and continue to whisk until smooth. Allow the sauce to cool in the pan before storing in a glass container in the fridge. Drizzle over matzo or dip a piece of matzo straight into the sauce.

ENTRÉES

LOWER EAST SIDE FRIED CHICKEN . . . 69

CHARRED LEMON BRAISED CHICKEN . . . 70

WHITE MATZO PIZZA WITH
POTATOES AND SMOKED GRUYÈRE . . . 72

PESTO CAPRESE MATZO PIZZA . . . 74

MATZO SPANAKOPITA . . . 75

ANYTIME BRISKET WITH MATZO SPAETZLE . . . 79

MATZO TACOS WITH YESTERDAY'S BRISKET . . . 82

QUINOA FALAFEL WITH SPICED YOGURT SAUCE . . . 84

MATZO MUSTARD-CRUSTED SALMON . . . 87

COD CAKES WITH REMOULADE SAUCE . . . 88

MEAT LOAF WITH CHARRED-TOMATO GLAZE . . . 91

LOWER EAST SIDE
FRIED CHICKEN

1 quart nondairy creamer

Juice and grated zest of 1 lemon

2 tablespoons kosher salt, plus more to taste

2 garlic cloves, finely chopped

1 tablespoon hot sauce (such as Tabasco)

1 chicken (2 to 3 pounds), cut into 8 pieces

4 large egg whites

DREDGE

1 cup matzo cake meal

1 cup matzo meal

1½ tablespoons garlic powder

1 tablespoon onion powder

¼ teaspoon cayenne

½ teaspoon kosher salt

Neutral oil, for frying

Honey, for serving (optional)

TIP Do not fill the pot more than halfway with oil, as the oil will boil up when the chicken is added.

Surprise your seder guests by serving them fried chicken and you'll definitely have to add more chairs around the table next year! Brining is key to keeping the chicken moist and seasoning it all the way to the bone. This version uses a buttermilk-style brine made with nondairy creamer to tenderize the meat, keeping it kosher for Passover. It should marinate for at least twelve hours. The matzo meal dredge provides the perfect crunchy crust to the finished fried chicken.

SERVES 4 TO 6

1 In a large airtight container or zip-top plastic bag, combine the creamer, lemon juice and zest, the 2 tablespoons salt, garlic, and hot sauce. Add the chicken, turn to coat, and marinate in the refrigerator for at least 12 hours.

2 Remove the chicken from the brine and dry well with paper towels. (Discard the brine.) In a large bowl, beat the egg whites until frothy. In a separate large bowl, mix all the ingredients for the dredge. Dip each piece of chicken into the egg whites, letting any excess drip off, then into the dredge, pressing to adhere. Place on a baking sheet and let sit for 15 minutes, until the crust begins to soften.

3 Meanwhile, heat about 5 inches of oil (see Tip), to 350°F in a deep pot fitted with a deep-fry thermometer. (If you don't have a thermometer, use the wooden spoon method on page 26.) Line a plate with paper towels. Working in batches, fry the chicken until golden brown and crisp; the white meat will take 8 to 10 minutes and the dark meat, 10 to 12 minutes. Transfer to the paper towel–lined plate to drain and season lightly with salt.

4 Serve the chicken warm, at room temperature, or even cold, straight from the refrigerator. A little drizzle of honey right before eating adds a great Southern-inspired twist.

CHARRED LEMON
BRAISED CHICKEN

2 tablespoons neutral oil

3 lemons, halved crosswise

4 pounds chicken thighs and legs, bone-in, skin on

Kosher salt and freshly ground black pepper

2 fennel bulbs, cut into large dice (2 cups)

1 yellow onion, cut into large dice (1 cup)

3 garlic cloves, peeled and smashed

¼ cup white wine

1 teaspoon potato starch

2 cups chicken stock, store-bought or homemade (page 32)

2 bay leaves

CRUMBS

½ cup extra-virgin olive oil

1 garlic clove, grated

1½ cups matzo farfel, coarsely chopped or pulsed into crumbs

Kosher salt and freshly ground black pepper

¼ cup finely chopped fresh flat-leaf parsley

The way we incorporated the farfel crumbs into this dish is reminiscent of how you make classic French cassoulet. By adding them to the dish in two stages, we build a thicker, crunchier layer on top. Then, when the chicken is served, some of the farfel crumbs that softened in the braising liquid mix with the fennel and onion and give the feel of traditional stuffing. This dish is a fantastic one-pot meal.

SERVES 4

1 Place a rack in the center of the oven and preheat the oven to 400°F. Heat 1 tablespoon of the oil in a large, heavy-bottomed, ovenproof pot over medium-high heat. When the oil begins to smoke, add the lemons, cut side down, and sear until deep golden brown, 3 minutes. Transfer to a plate and set aside.

2 Season the chicken liberally with salt and pepper. Add the remaining 1 tablespoon oil to the same pan and heat over medium-high heat. When it begins to shimmer, add the chicken, skin side down, in a single layer, working in batches if needed. Sear until the skin is golden brown and crispy, 5 minutes per side. Reduce the heat if the skin darkens too quickly, but do not rush this step as it will ensure the skin is not chewy after the braise. Set the seared chicken aside.

3 Pour off any excess fat, leaving about 2 tablespoons in the pot, and set over medium-high heat. When the oil begins to shimmer, add the fennel, onion, and garlic and cook without stirring, 3 minutes, until golden and roasted on one side. Then stir and add the white wine to deglaze the pan. Continue to cook for 1 minute.

4 Combine the potato starch and chicken stock in a small bowl. Once the starch has dissolved, pour the mixture into the pot with the vegetables, add the bay leaves, and bring the braising liquid to a boil. Squeeze the juice from the charred lemon halves into the braising liquid, then drop in the rinds as well.

5 Add the chicken back to the braising liquid, submerging it halfway. Transfer the pot to the oven and cook for 20 minutes, until the chicken is halfway cooked and the liquid has started to thicken.

6 Meanwhile, make the garlic farfel crumbs. Line a plate with paper towels. Heat the olive oil in a large skillet over medium heat. When it begins to shimmer, add the garlic and cook until fragrant, 30 seconds. Add the farfel crumbs, season with salt and pepper, and sauté, stirring often, until the farfel is golden brown, 6 minutes. Transfer to the paper towel–lined plate to drain. Allow the crumbs to cool fully, then mix in the parsley. (You can make the crumbs, without the parsley, in advance; they'll stay fresh in an airtight container for up to 1 week, then just add the parsley before using.)

7 Open the oven and sprinkle half of the farfel crumbs evenly across the surface of the braising chicken. Continue cooking until the chicken is tender and cooked through, another 20 minutes. Remove the chicken, set the oven to broil, and sprinkle the remaining crumbs on top. Return to the middle rack and broil until the farfel crumbs and chicken skin crisp up, 1 minute more. Allow the braised chicken to rest in the pot for 5 minutes before serving.

MASHUGANA madman, crazy person, lunatic

WHITE MATZO PIZZA
WITH POTATOES
AND SMOKED GRUYÈRE

SAUCE

2 tablespoons unsalted butter

1 tablespoon potato starch

1 cup whole milk

½ cup grated Parmesan cheese

⅓ teaspoon grated nutmeg

½ teaspoon kosher salt

PIZZA

1 pound red potatoes

4 sheets of matzo

4 teaspoons extra-virgin olive oil

½ pound smoked Gruyère cheese, grated

White truffle oil, for drizzling (optional)

1 tablespoon finely chopped fresh chives

This recipe is meant to make you think about all the ways matzo pizzas can be made throughout the year. The earthy, funky Gruyère with creamy potatoes is a timeless combination that simply works! When it's not Passover, a few drops of white truffle oil to finish the pizza is a delicious touch. **SERVES 4**

1 Melt the butter in a small pot over medium heat. Whisk in the potato starch. Slowly pour in the milk and bring to a simmer, whisking continuously to prevent the sauce from becoming lumpy and sticking to the bottom of the pot. Simmer until the milk has thickened and the starchy flavor has cooked out, 3 minutes. Remove the pan from the heat.

2 Whisk the Parmesan, nutmeg, and salt into the sauce. Transfer to a small heatproof bowl, cover with a piece of plastic wrap directly on the surface to prevent a skin from forming, and refrigerate until fully cooled, about 20 minutes.

3 Meanwhile, place the red potatoes in a medium pot and cover with cold salted water. Bring to a boil over high heat, then reduce the heat to medium-low and simmer until just fork-tender, 20 minutes. Using a slotted spoon, remove and set aside until cool enough to handle, about 10 minutes. Cut into ¼-inch-thick slices.

4 Place a rack in the center of the oven and preheat the broiler. Working in batches if needed, lay the matzo sheets pale side up on a baking sheet and brush the top of each with 1 teaspoon olive oil. Toast in the oven until golden brown, 1 to 2 minutes. Remove from the oven and set aside.

5 Spread the toasted side of each matzo with ¼ cup of the sauce. Place the potato slices on top and sprinkle with the Gruyère. Return the matzos to the oven and broil until the cheese melts and starts to brown, and the sauce begins to bubble around the edges, 2 minutes. Drizzle the finished pizzas with the truffle oil, if using, and sprinkle with the chives. Cut each pizza into quarters and serve.

TIP Even though neither truffles nor oil breaks any of the basic kosher for Passover rules, no agency currently certifies any truffle oil on the market as acceptable.

PESTO CAPRESE
MATZO PIZZA

2 cups fresh basil leaves

1 garlic clove

½ cup grated Parmesan cheese, plus
more for serving

½ cup plus 4 teaspoons extra-virgin
olive oil

½ cup pine nuts, toasted

Kosher salt and freshly ground
black pepper

4 sheets of matzo

1¾ cups shredded mozzarella

1 large tomato, thinly sliced

KIBITZ meddle or gossip

Here, we took the classic Italian pizza made with mozzarella cheese, tomatoes, and fresh basil and amped it up. The basil became pesto and the matzo stood in for the crust. Matzo adds crunch that regular dough just can't beat. **SERVES 4**

1 Make the pesto: Add the basil, garlic, Parmesan, ½ cup olive oil, and ¼ cup of the pine nuts to a food processor. Pulse until smooth. Season with salt and pepper and set aside.

2 Place a rack in the center of the oven and preheat the broiler. Working in batches if needed, lay the matzo sheets pale side up on a baking sheet and brush the top of each with 1 teaspoon olive oil. Transfer to the oven and toast until golden brown, 1 to 2 minutes. Remove and set aside.

3 Cover each toasted matzo with ¼ cup plus 1 tablespoon of the mozzarella. Return to the oven and broil until the cheese has melted, about 1 minute. Remove and spread each matzo with ¼ cup pesto, covering the melted cheese. Lay the tomato slices on top and sprinkle with the remaining ½ cup mozzarella. Transfer back to the oven to broil until the cheese has melted and starts to brown a bit, 1 minute more.

4 Sprinkle the finished pizzas with the remaining ¼ cup pine nuts. Cut each pizza into quarters and serve with more grated Parmesan on top.

MATZO
SPANAKOPITA

SAUCE

4 tablespoons (½ stick) unsalted butter

2 tablespoons potato starch

2 cups whole milk

½ cup grated Parmesan cheese

¼ teaspoon grated nutmeg

1 teaspoon kosher salt

SPANAKOPITA

3 tablespoons extra-virgin olive oil

1 cup sliced shallots

1 garlic clove, thinly sliced

1 pound fresh spinach or 1 10-ounce package frozen chopped spinach, thawed and squeezed dry (see Tip, page 76)

Kosher salt and freshly ground black pepper

3 large eggs

1 teaspoon grated lemon zest (from 1 lemon)

4 sheets of matzo

½ cup grated Parmesan cheese

¾ cup crumbled feta cheese

½ cup pine nuts, toasted

Our version of matzo "lasagna" gets the Greek treatment when married with the classic spinach pie. Here, matzo replaces the commonly used phyllo dough, giving the spanakopita heartiness and crunch, and coming closer to how it is prepared on the Greek islands. Serve it as a dairy side dish or a great vegetarian entrée. You may find you like this version even more than the traditional one! **SERVES 4 TO 6**

1 To make the sauce, melt the butter in a small pot over medium heat. Whisk in the potato starch. Slowly pour in the milk and bring to a simmer, whisking continuously to prevent the sauce from becoming lumpy and sticking to the bottom of the pot. Simmer until the milk has thickened and the starchy flavor has cooked out, 3 minutes. Remove the pan from the heat.

2 Whisk the Parmesan cheese, nutmeg, and salt into the sauce. Transfer to a small heatproof bowl, cover with a piece of plastic wrap directly on the surface to prevent a skin from forming, and refrigerate until fully cooled, about 20 minutes.

3 Preheat the oven to 400°F. Line a colander with a clean kitchen towel and set in the sink. Brush an 8-inch square baking dish with 1 tablespoon of the olive oil.

4 Heat the remaining 2 tablespoons olive oil in a large pot over medium-low heat. When it begins to shimmer, add the shallots and garlic and cook until soft and translucent, 5 minutes. Add the spinach, season with salt and pepper, and cover. Cook the spinach, stirring occasionally, until wilted, 6 minutes. Pour the vegetable mixture into the colander and use the kitchen towel to squeeze out as much moisture as possible. Set aside to cool.

recipe continues

5 Remove the cooled sauce from the refrigerator and whisk in the eggs. Stir the lemon zest into the spinach mixture. Lay one sheet of matzo in the bottom of the prepared baking dish. Cover with ½ cup sauce, then spread 1 cup of the spinach mixture over the sauce. Sprinkle with 1 tablespoon of the Parmesan, 3 tablespoons of the feta, and 3 tablespoons of the pine nuts. Place another sheet of matzo on top, pressing down gently. Repeat the layers, then cover the final sheet of matzo with the remaining sauce, Parmesan, and feta.

6 Transfer to the oven and bake until the feta on top turns golden brown, the sauce puffs up, and the matzo softens, 30 to 35 minutes. Remove and allow the pie to rest for 10 minutes before slicing.

TIP If using frozen spinach, add it to the pan with the sautéed shallots and garlic and cook until the spinach is dry and the mixture is evenly combined, about 2 minutes. Season with salt and pepper to taste and set aside to cool before incorporating into the recipe.

 a good person

ANYTIME BRISKET
~WITH~ MATZO SPAETZLE

1 point-cut brisket (also known as "second cut"), 3 to 4 pounds, fat cap trimmed to ⅛ inch

Kosher salt and freshly ground black pepper

3 tablespoons neutral oil

3 yellow onions, thinly sliced (3 cups)

3 garlic cloves, thinly sliced

2 bay leaves

5 sprigs of fresh thyme, tied with twine

½ cup tomato paste (4 ounces)

2 cups dry red wine, such as Pinot Noir or Cabernet Sauvignon

1 quart chicken stock, store-bought or homemade (page 32)

¾ pound whole carrots, 1½-inch diameter

2 tablespoons extra-virgin olive oil

Matzo Spaetzle (page 81)

2 tablespoons thinly sliced fresh chives

This brisket is the perfect comfort food for any occasion. The sauce is sweet and tangy and helps capture the flavor of the old school dish that was a favorite part of countless childhoods. The brisket cut is made up of two distinct muscles. For this recipe, we ask our butcher for point-cut brisket instead of the traditional flat cut, as it contains much better marbling to keep the brisket moist during its long cooking time. The brisket can be served the same day it is braised, but we prefer to slice the meat when it's cold and heat it up the next day. The brisket will stay fresh for up to four days in the refrigerator or for months if wrapped tightly and frozen. SERVES 6 TO 8

1 Preheat the oven to 325°F.

2 Liberally season the brisket with salt and pepper. Heat 2 tablespoons of the neutral oil in a large Dutch oven over high heat. When it just begins to smoke, lay the brisket fat side down and sear until well browned, 5 to 7 minutes. Flip and brown the other side for 5 minutes more. Remove the brisket from the pan and set aside.

recipe continues

TIP If you don't have a Dutch oven, you can sear the brisket and make the gravy in a large saucepan, then transfer the meat to a roasting pan, pour the boiling braising liquid over it, and cover with foil before cooking in the oven.

3 Heat the remaining 1 tablespoon of neutral oil in the same pan over medium heat. When it begins to smoke, add the onion, garlic, and bay leaves. Cook, stirring often, until the onions begin to caramelize, 8 to 9 minutes. Add the thyme bundle and tomato paste and cook, stirring, until the onions are evenly coated and the tomato paste darkens, 1 minute. Add the wine and cook until reduced by one-third, about 5 minutes. Add the stock, increase the heat to high, bring to a boil, and nestle the brisket back into the braising liquid. Cover and transfer to the oven.

4 After 2½ hours, remove the lid and add the carrots to the braising liquid. Continue to cook for 30 minutes more, until the carrots and the brisket are just fork-tender with a little resistance. Remove from the oven, discard the bay leaves and thyme bundle, and allow the brisket to cool to room temperature in the braising liquid. Then cover loosely with aluminum foil and refrigerate overnight.

5 To serve: Preheat the oven to 350°F. Spoon off any congealed fat from the onion gravy and discard. Remove the brisket from the gravy and cut against the grain into ¼-inch slices. Remove the carrots and cut into 2-inch pieces. Place the brisket and carrots in a 4-quart casserole dish and pour the gravy over. Cover the dish with foil and place in the oven to warm through, 30 to 45 minutes.

6 Meanwhile, heat the olive oil in a large skillet over medium-high heat. Add the spaetzle and cook, stirring often, until warmed through, 2 to 3 minutes. Mix the chives into the spaetzle and serve with the brisket and the remaining gravy in a bowl alongside.

MATZO SPAETZLE

MAKES 4 CUPS

2 cups matzo cake meal

4 large eggs

2 teaspoons kosher salt

1 cup chicken stock, store-bought or
    homemade (page 32)

⅛ teaspoon grated nutmeg

1 Bring a large pot of salted
water to a boil over high heat.
Make an ice bath in a large
bowl and set near the stove.

2 In a medium bowl, mix the cake
meal, eggs, salt, stock, and nutmeg
until a smooth, sticky dough forms.
Set a colander with ¼-inch holes (or
a spaetzle maker) over the boiling
water and, using a rubber spatula,
push one-third of the dough at a
time through the holes into the pot.
The spaetzle will instantly float.
Stir them around to prevent them
from sticking together. Cook for
45 seconds before scooping them
into the ice bath. Repeat with the
remaining dough. Drain the spaetzle
well and store in an airtight container
in the refrigerator for up to 3 days.

MATZO TACOS
ᴡɪᴛʜ YESTERDAY'S BRISKET

TORTILLAS

2 cups matzo meal

1½ cups warm water

2 tablespoons extra-virgin olive oil

1 teaspoon kosher salt

18 ounces cooked brisket, cut into 1-inch pieces (page 79)

2 cups salsa, store-bought or homemade (page 49), plus more for serving

¼ cup fresh cilantro leaves

Pickled Onions (page 45; optional)

Talk about an inspiring way to use leftovers! Take what's remaining of that tender brisket and give your main course another life. Making these fresh matzo meal tortillas takes some practice, but once you get them down they are sure to become a go-to.

SERVES 4 (MAKES 12 TORTILLAS)

1 In a medium bowl, stir together the matzo meal, warm water, olive oil, and salt until a smooth dough forms. Allow the dough to rest, uncovered, for 5 minutes. Then, using your hands, form ¼ cup of dough into a flat disc. Repeat with the remaining dough. Place each disc between two sheets of plastic wrap and use a rolling pin to roll it into a 7-inch circle about ¼ inch thick.

2 Heat a small nonstick skillet or griddle over medium-high heat. When it just begins to smoke, place 1 tortilla in the pan and cook until some dark brown spots appear, about 30 seconds. Use a spatula to flip it and cook for another 30 seconds. Transfer to a wire rack to cool and repeat with the remaining tortillas. It is OK to stack the cooked tortillas.

3 Place the brisket and salsa in a medium saucepan over medium heat, cover, and gently simmer until warmed through, about 10 minutes.

4 Serve the brisket in the tortillas, topped with cilantro leaves, pickled onions, if desired, and additional salsa.

TIP The cooked tortillas feel stiff and brittle when they are removed from the pan, but as they cool and rest they will soften and become pliable. Stored in an airtight zip-top bag, they will keep for about 1 week at room temperature.

QUINOA FALAFEL
WITH SPICED YOGURT SAUCE

PARVE
(DAIRY WHEN SERVED
WITH YOGURT)

¼ cup extra-virgin olive oil

1 red onion, finely diced (1 cup)

2 garlic cloves

1½ teaspoons ground cumin

¼ teaspoon dried red pepper flakes

½ cup matzo meal

1 large egg, beaten

1 cup cooked quinoa

1 teaspoon grated lemon zest

1 teaspoon kosher salt

½ cup finely chopped fresh flat-leaf parsley

⅓ cup finely chopped fresh cilantro

⅓ cup finely chopped fresh mint

Neutral oil for greasing the baking sheet

3 tablespoons matzo cake meal

2 cups mixed greens

Spiced Yogurt Sauce (recipe follows; optional)

This aromatic, family-friendly dish is packed with exotic spices and protein. Quinoa takes the place of the usual chickpeas and the uncooked patties are still perfect even after being stored in the refrigerator overnight. The spiced yogurt is a great acidic counterpart to the nutty falafel, but a spicy aioli can be a great dairy-free substitute, too. You might find yourself making these for Passover, a picnic, or a weeknight dinner. Serve them over a hearty green salad, and you have a complete meal. SERVES 4

1 Heat 2 tablespoons of the olive oil in a large skillet over medium heat. When the oil begins to shimmer, add the onion, garlic, cumin, and red pepper flakes and sauté until soft and translucent, 3 minutes. Transfer the mixture to a plate to cool.

2 In a small bowl, combine the matzo meal, remaining 2 tablespoons olive oil, egg, and 3 tablespoons water. In a large bowl combine the quinoa, lemon zest, salt, parsley, cilantro, mint, onion mixture, and matzo meal mixture. Stir together and refrigerate, uncovered, for 15 minutes.

3 Meanwhile, position a rack near the bottom of the oven and preheat the oven to 475°F. Using a neutral oil, grease a baking sheet.

4 Remove the falafel mixture from the refrigerator and add the cake meal, 1 tablespoon at a time, until the mixture holds together when squeezed. Using your hands, form 2-inch patties ½ inch thick and place on the oiled baking sheet. Set on the lowest rack and bake until a golden brown crust forms on the bottom, 10 minutes. Flip and continue cooking until the other side is browned, another 10 minutes. Serve over mixed greens with the spiced yogurt, if desired.

SPICED YOGURT SAUCE

MAKES 1 CUP

1 cup Greek yogurt

¼ teaspoon ground cinnamon

½ teaspoon ground cumin

½ teaspoon ground coriander

½ teaspoon hot paprika

3 tablespoons chopped fresh mint

Juice and grated zest of ½ lemon

¼ teaspoon kosher salt

Combine all the ingredients in a small bowl. Store in an airtight container in the refrigerator up to 1 week.

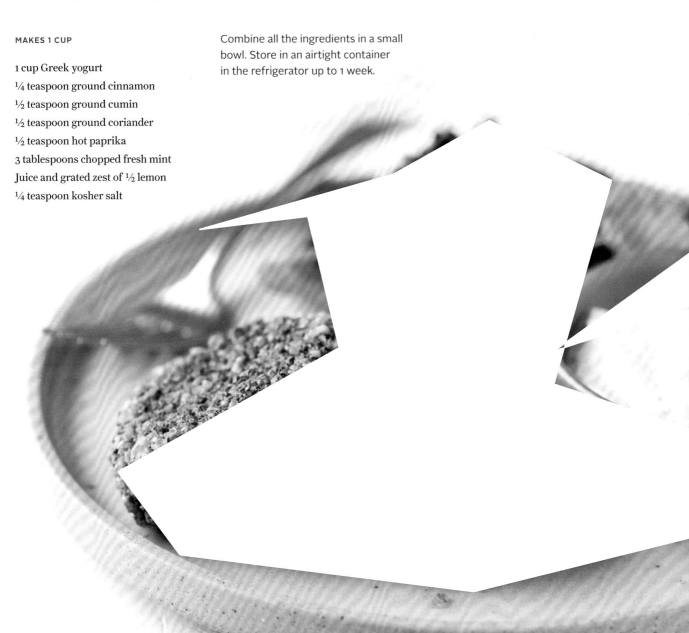

MATZO MUSTARD-CRUSTED
SALMON

4 teaspoons extra-virgin olive oil, plus more for greasing the pan

¼ cup Greek yogurt

2 tablespoons Dijon mustard

Kosher salt and freshly ground black pepper

½ cup matzo meal

1 tablespoon grated lemon zest (from 1 lemon)

¼ cup chopped fresh herbs (tarragon, parsley, chives)

4 5-ounce skinless salmon fillets

Lemon wedges (optional)

SCHMATTA rags

This dish is simple, easy, and great for every season. The matzo meal crust is flavorful and light, and the mustard-yogurt marinade acts as a built-in sauce.　**SERVES 4**

1　Position one rack in the top third of the oven and another in the center. Preheat the oven to 400°F. Line a baking sheet with aluminum foil and lightly oil.

2　In a small bowl, mix the yogurt and mustard and season lightly with salt and pepper. In a separate small bowl, mix the matzo meal, lemon zest, herbs, and olive oil. Season with salt and pepper.

3　Season both sides of the salmon fillets with salt and pepper and place on the prepared baking sheet, skinned side down. Spread the mustard-yogurt mixture evenly over the tops. Sprinkle with the matzo meal mixture. Place on the center oven rack and bake until barely warm in the middle and halfway cooked, 6 to 7 minutes.

4　Remove the salmon from the oven and preheat the broiler. When it is hot, place the salmon on the top rack and broil until the crust is golden brown and the flesh is just cooked through, 2 to 3 minutes. Serve with lemon wedges, if desired.

COD CAKES
 WITH **REMOULADE SAUCE**

1½ pounds skinless cod fillets

Kosher salt and freshly ground
black pepper

2 tablespoons extra-virgin olive oil

1 large russet potato, peeled and
cubed (1½ cups)

1 small onion, diced (½ cup)

1 garlic clove, minced

2 large eggs, beaten

½ cup thinly sliced scallions, green
part only

3 tablespoons chopped fresh flat-leaf
parsley

½ cup matzo meal

¼ cup neutral oil

Remoulade Sauce (page 90)

Lemon wedges (optional)

Inspired by my summers spent in Denmark, these light, flaky cakes are delicate, with a crisp coating, yet hearty from the potato. The vibrant sauce is the perfect accompaniment. You can also serve these cakes as a first course or a side.   **SERVES 4**

1 Preheat the oven to 350°F. Line a baking sheet with aluminum foil.

2 Place the cod fillets on the lined baking sheet. Season both sides with salt and pepper and brush with 1 tablespoon of the olive oil. Bake until the fish is cooked through, 10 to 12 minutes, depending on the thickness of the fillets. Keep the oven on and transfer the fish to a plate to cool completely. Break the cooled cod into large pieces; it will naturally flake apart.

3 Meanwhile, place the potato in a small pot and cover with cold salted water. Bring to a boil over high heat, then reduce the heat to medium-low and simmer until tender, about 15 minutes. Drain well, mash the potato with a fork, and set aside to cool.

4 Heat the remaining 1 tablespoon of olive oil in a small skillet over medium heat. When it begins to shimmer, add the onion and garlic and cook until soft and translucent, 2 minutes. Transfer to a plate to cool for about 5 minutes. In a large bowl, whisk together the eggs, scallions, parsley, and onion mixture. Add the cod, mashed potato, and matzo meal to the egg mixture and gently fold together using a rubber spatula, taking care not to break up the fish further. Season with 1 teaspoon salt and some pepper, cover the bowl with plastic wrap, and chill in the refrigerator for 10 minutes.

5 Line the baking sheet from the cod with fresh aluminum foil. Use a ⅓-cup measure to scoop portions of the cod mixture. With

damp hands, form into 2½-inch patties about 1 inch thick. Place on the prepared baking sheet.

6   Heat 2 tablespoons of the neutral oil in a large skillet over medium-high heat. When it begins to shimmer, add the patties in a single layer, working in batches as needed, and cook until golden brown, 2 to 3 minutes per side. Return the cod cakes to the baking sheet and bake until warmed through, about 5 minutes. Serve with the remoulade sauce and lemon wedges, if desired.

REMOULADE SAUCE

MAKES ¾ CUP

½ cup mayonnaise

1 tablespoon finely chopped shallots

2 tablespoons chopped dill pickles
   (or dill relish)

2 teaspoons fresh lemon juice

1 tablespoon Dijon mustard

⅛ teaspoon cayenne

1 tablespoon ketchup

Combine all the ingredients in a small bowl. Store in an airtight container in the refrigerator for up to 1 week.

Serious study.

MEAT LOAF
WITH CHARRED-TOMATO GLAZE

GLAZE

4 plum tomatoes, halved lengthwise

1 tablespoon neutral oil

3 tablespoons (packed) brown sugar

3 tablespoons apple cider vinegar

1 8-ounce can tomato sauce

MEAT LOAF

3 tablespoons extra-virgin olive oil

2 yellow onions, chopped (2 cups)

2 carrots, grated (1 cup)

2 garlic cloves, thinly sliced

2 teaspoons chopped fresh thyme

1 cup matzo meal

½ cup beef broth

2 pounds ground beef chuck

2 large eggs, beaten

¼ cup chopped fresh flat-leaf parsley

2 teaspoons kosher salt

1 teaspoon freshly ground black pepper

This is a classic meat loaf with a quick homemade ketchup-style glaze. It's perfect for dinner any day of the week and even better the next day as a sandwich. Nothing fancy schmancy, but who doesn't love comfort food? **SERVES 4 TO 6**

1 Place a rack in the upper third of the oven and preheat the broiler.

2 Make the glaze: In a medium bowl, toss the tomatoes with the neutral oil. Lay them on a baking sheet, skin side up. Char under the broiler until the skins have blackened, 15 minutes. Transfer the tomatoes to a food processor with the brown sugar, vinegar, and tomato sauce and pulse until smooth. Pour the glaze into a small pot, set over medium heat, and simmer until it has reduced by half and thickened, about 30 minutes. Set aside to cool.

3 Meanwhile, reduce the oven temperature to 350°F. Heat 2 tablespoons of the olive oil in a large skillet over medium-high heat. When it begins to shimmer, add the onion, carrot, garlic, and thyme and sauté until the vegetables are soft and lightly browned, 9 minutes. Transfer to a plate to cool.

4 In a large bowl, mix ½ cup of the matzo meal with the beef broth and let it sit to hydrate, 10 minutes. Add the sautéed vegetables, ¼ cup of the glaze, the ground beef, remaining ½ cup matzo meal, eggs, parsley, salt, and pepper and stir until just combined.

5 Grease a 9 × 5-inch loaf pan with the remaining 1 tablespoon of olive oil. Add the meat mixture, rounding the top with your hands. Coat the top of the meat loaf with ¼ cup of the charred-tomato glaze. Bake until the glaze has turned deep red and the meat loaf is cooked through, 60 minutes. Remove the meat loaf from the oven and allow to rest in the pan for 10 minutes before slicing. Serve the remaining glaze alongside.

DESSERTS

CHOCOLATE CARAMEL MATZO CRUNCH
WITH CANDIED GINGER . . . 94

ROCKY ROAD TRUFFLES . . . 97

CHOCOLATE CHIP COOKIES . . . 98

PIZZARELLE . . . 101

MATZO TIRAMISU . . . 102

APPLE CRUMB PIE . . . 105

CHOCOLATE-CHERRY TORTE . . . 107

CHOCOLATE CARAMEL
MATZO CRUNCH CANDIED GINGER

DAIRY
(PARVE, IF USING
MARGARINE AND DAIRY-
FREE CHOCOLATE)

5 sheets of matzo

1 cup (packed) dark brown sugar

8 tablespoons (1 stick) butter or margarine

1 cup semisweet chocolate chips (6 ounces)

¼ cup chopped crystallized ginger

1 teaspoon flaky sea salt, such as Maldon or fleur de sel

Most people have a recipe for matzo brittle that has been passed down for generations. Ours separates itself from the pack with the addition of candied ginger and flaky sea salt. This is an ideal hostess gift to bring to any seder! **MAKES 30 PIECES OF CANDY**

1 Preheat the oven to 375°F. Line a rimmed baking sheet with aluminum foil, then cover with a piece of parchment.

2 Lay the matzos over the baking sheet, covering it completely. You will need to break some into smaller pieces.

3 Melt the brown sugar and butter in a small pot over medium heat, stirring constantly with a rubber spatula, until the mixture comes to a boil, 3 minutes. Cook, stirring, for 3 minutes more, until the caramel has thickened and turned deep amber. Remove the pot from the heat and immediately pour the mixture over the matzos to cover them completely.

4 Place the baking sheet in the oven and reduce the temperature

to 350°F. Bake for 15 minutes, checking every few minutes to be sure the caramel is not burning. If the caramel starts to get too dark, remove the baking sheet from the oven, reduce the heat to 325°F, return the baking sheet to the oven, and continue baking.

5 Remove the baking sheet from the oven and immediately sprinkle with the chocolate chips. Let stand for 5 minutes to melt, then use a spatula to spread the chocolate over the matzos. Sprinkle with the ginger and sea salt. Place the sheet in the freezer or refrigerator until fully set, 20 to 30 minutes. Break the matzo crunch into large pieces and store in an airtight container at room temperature or in the refrigerator, if you prefer it cold.

SCHMALTZY corny, over the top

ROCKY ROAD
TRUFFLES

PARVE
(DAIRY IF USING
MILK CHOCOLATE
AND BUTTER)

1 cup matzo farfel

1 cup walnut or pecan pieces

12 ounces dark chocolate chips or chopped chocolate

2½ teaspoons margarine or butter

½ cup plain unsweetened almond milk

¾ cup mini marshmallows

1 tablespoon flaky sea salt, such as Maldon or fleur de sel

These chocolate truffles are the perfect Passover candy. Toasted farfel and marshmallows make for a richly textured interior, and the coating of nuts and a bit of sea salt add the perfect crunch on the outside. **MAKES ABOUT 36 TRUFFLES**

1 Preheat the oven to 350°F.

2 Line two baking sheets with aluminum foil; spread the farfel on one sheet and the nuts on the other. Place both sheets in the oven and bake until the farfel and nuts are lightly toasted and aromatic, about 2 minutes. Remove from the oven, roughly chop the nuts, and set both aside.

3 Combine the chocolate, margarine, and almond milk in a saucepan over medium heat. Stir constantly with a rubber spatula until the chocolate has melted and the mixture is smooth. Pour the chocolate mixture into a large bowl and set aside for 15 minutes to cool.

Fold in the marshmallows and farfel. Place the bowl in the refrigerator to chill and thicken, about 1 hour.

4 Line a baking sheet with parchment paper. Measure out 2 teaspoons of the chocolate mixture and, using your hands, roll it into a ball. Roll through the chopped nuts to coat and set on the prepared baking sheet. Repeat with the remaining chocolate mixture and nuts. Sprinkle a small pinch of sea salt on top of each truffle. Return the truffles to the refrigerator to firm up, about 1 hour. Store in an airtight container at room temperature for 2 to 3 weeks or in the freezer for up to 3 months.

SCHLEP pull, drag, tug, yank

CHOCOLATE CHIP
COOKIES

1 cup matzo cake meal

¼ cup matzo meal

¼ cup potato starch

¾ teaspoon baking soda

1 teaspoon kosher salt

16 tablespoons (2 sticks) unsalted butter, room temperature

1 cup granulated sugar

⅔ cup (packed) light brown sugar

2 teaspoons vanilla extract

2 large eggs

2 cups chocolate chips

We always had macaroons on our seder table, of course—Streit's macaroons, straight from the can. But for a fantastic homemade alternative, we urge you to try these amazing cookies. They will make you rethink what a "Passover cookie" can be. **MAKES ABOUT 50 COOKIES**

1 Place a rack in the middle of the oven and preheat the oven to 375°F. Line two baking sheets with parchment paper.

2 In a small bowl, whisk together the matzo cake meal, matzo meal, potato starch, baking soda, and salt.

3 In a stand mixer fitted with the paddle attachment, beat the butter on medium speed until light and fluffy, 1 minute. Add the granulated and brown sugars and beat for 2 minutes, scraping down the sides as needed with a rubber spatula. Add the vanilla, beating until combined, then add the eggs one at a time, beating for 1 minute after each to incorporate. Reduce the speed to low and add the dry ingredients in three batches. Fold in the chocolate chips.

4 Using a 1-tablespoon measure, scoop the batter onto the prepared baking sheets, leaving 2 to 3 inches between cookies—they will spread during baking. Bake one sheet at a time until the cookies are evenly golden brown, 8 to 10 minutes, rotating the sheet after 4 minutes. Remove from the oven and let the cookies rest on the baking sheet for 1 minute, then transfer to a wire rack to cool. Repeat with the remaining dough, cooling the baking sheets between batches. Once the cookies have fully cooled, store them in an airtight container for up to 2 weeks.

PIZZARELLE

3 large eggs, separated

¼ teaspoon kosher salt

1 tablespoon extra-virgin olive oil

1 teaspoon grated lemon zest

¼ cup sugar

¾ cup matzo meal

⅓ cup raisins

⅓ cup pine nuts, toasted

Neutral oil, for frying

Honey, for serving (optional)

Pizzarelle is a popular Roman Passover cookie that is really more of a fritter with pine nuts and honey. Airy and lumpy before frying, the end result is a glorious ruin from culinary tradition that spans many centuries and many influences—Roman, Spanish, Libyan, and Sicilian. SERVES 4 TO 6

1 In a small bowl, whisk together the egg yolks, salt, olive oil, and lemon zest. In a stand mixer fitted with the whisk attachment or in a medium bowl with a whisk, beat the egg whites until foamy. Add the sugar and continue to beat until the whites are shiny and have stiff peaks.

2 Use a rubber spatula to fold the egg whites into the egg yolk mixture, then fold in the matzo meal, followed by the raisins and the pine nuts.

3 Line a plate with paper towels. Pour at least 2 inches of neutral oil into a large pot fitted with a deep-fry thermometer and heat to 350°F over medium-high heat. (If you don't have a deep-fry thermometer, see the wooden spoon test on page 26.) Working in batches, use 2 large spoons to shape 2 tablespoons into a football shape, then gently drop the fritter into the oil. Repeat with the remaining dough and fry until golden brown, 1 to 2 minutes per side. Use a spider or slotted spoon to remove the fritters and transfer to the paper towel–lined plate to drain.

4 Serve warm or at room temperature, drizzled with honey, if desired.

BASHERT one's beloved, meant to be

TIP When frying, don't overcrowd the pot or the oil temperature will drop and the pizzarelle will become greasy.

MATZO
TIRAMISU

7 large egg yolks

½ cup sugar

⅓ cup plus 2 tablespoons sweet Marsala wine

8 ounces cream cheese

1 cup heavy cream

1 cup brewed coffee or espresso

¼ cup rum

5 sheets of matzo, broken into 2-inch pieces

2 tablespoons unsweetened Dutch-process cocoa powder

Tiramisu translates to "pick me up." And this popular Italian dessert sure lifts our mood! Here, we altered the classic by using matzos in place of traditional ladyfingers. The matzos soak up the cream, chocolate, and rum with mouthwatering results. **SERVES 6 TO 8**

1 Bring a large pot of water to a simmer over medium heat. Prepare an ice bath in a large bowl.

2 In a large heatproof bowl, whisk together the yolks and sugar. Using the simmering pot as a double boiler, set the bowl on top of the pot, being sure the water doesn't touch the bottom of the bowl, and whisk until the sugar dissolves. Add the ⅓ cup Marsala and continue to whisk until the mixture is thick, has doubled in volume, and reads 150°F on a candy thermometer, about 10 minutes. If you don't have a thermometer, watch for the ribbon stage: The custard is ready once thick, pale-yellow ribbons form and hold their shape.

3 Remove the bowl from the heat and whisk in the cream cheese until fully incorporated. Set the bowl in the prepared ice bath, touching the water, and continue to whisk

until the custard begins to cool down, 3 to 4 minutes. Place plastic wrap directly on the surface of the custard to prevent a skin from forming. Let sit in the ice bath until fully cooled, about 20 minutes.

4 In a small bowl, stir together the remaining 2 tablespoons Marsala and the coffee and rum. In a medium bowl, whip the heavy cream to soft peaks. Fold the whipped cream into the marscarpone mixture to lighten. Add half the matzos and soak for 30 to 40 seconds, until they begin to soften. Arrange them in the bottom of an 8-inch square baking dish, then evenly spread with half the chilled custard. Soak the remaining matzos for 30 to 40 seconds, lay them over the first layer of custard, then top with the remaining custard. Evenly sift the cocoa powder over the top. Wrap the tiramisu with plastic wrap and refrigerate for at least 2 hours before serving.

APPLE
CRUMB PIE

PIECRUST

1½ cups matzo cake meal, plus more for dusting

½ cup (1 stick) margarine or vegetable shortening

½ teaspoon kosher salt

PIE FILLING

4 pounds baking apples (such as Gala, Pink Lady, or Granny Smith), peeled, cored, and sliced ¼ inch thick

2 tablespoons fresh lemon juice (from 1 lemon)

¾ cup sugar

2 tablespoons potato starch

¾ teaspoon kosher salt

½ teaspoon ground cinnamon

CRUMB TOPPING

¾ cup potato starch

½ cup matzo cake meal

2 tablespoons plus 2 teaspoons light brown sugar

1 teaspoon vanilla extract

½ teaspoon kosher salt

¼ cup neutral oil

Tired of eating meringue-based desserts on Passover? This apple pie delivers everything you look for in a traditional version: flaky crust, crunchy topping, scrumptious filling. This crust can be used to make everything from quiche to chicken pot pies.　SERVES 6 TO 8

1　Place a rack in the middle of the oven and preheat the oven to 375°F.

2　Make the crust: In a food processor, combine the matzo cake meal, margarine, and salt and pulse until pea-sized pieces form. With the motor running, slowly drizzle in ½ cup plus 1 tablespoon cold water until a ball of dough forms. Using your hands, form the dough into a flat disc, wrap with plastic, and refrigerate for at least 20 minutes.

3　Place a large sheet of parchment paper on a clean, dry surface. Dust the surface and a rolling pin with cake meal, then roll the dough into a 12-inch-wide circle. Lift the parchment paper and flip the dough into a 9-inch pie pan. Pinch any tears back together. Press the dough so that it sits flat along the corners and sides of the pie pan, then crimp the top edge around the pie.

4　Make the filling: In a large bowl, toss together the apples, lemon juice, sugar, potato starch, salt, and cinnamon until evenly coated. Place the apples in the piecrust, arranging them in even layers to avoid air pockets, and gently pushing down each layer as you fill the dish—it will seem like too many apples, but they will cook down. Bake for 45 minutes, until the crust turns golden brown and the apples have shrunk in volume by one-third.

recipe continues

5 Meanwhile, make the crumb topping: In a small bowl, combine the potato starch, cake meal, brown sugar, vanilla, and salt. Drizzle in the oil and use a fork to mix everything together until the crumbs are the size of peas.

6 Pull the pie from the oven, sprinkle the crumb topping over the apples, return to the oven, and continue to bake until the apple filling is soft and bubbling and the crust and crumb are both golden brown, 30 to 45 minutes more. Remove and allow the pie to cool to room temperature for at least 3 hours before slicing and serving. It will stay fresh, covered, at room temperature for up to 24 hours, or refrigerated for 4 days.

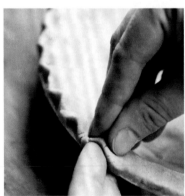

PLOTZ split, crack, burst, explode

CHOCOLATE-
CHERRY TORTE

PARVE
(DAIRY IF USING
MILK CHOCOLATE)

½ cup (1 stick) margarine, plus more for greasing the pan

8 ounces dark chocolate, chopped

5 large eggs, separated

¾ cup sugar

1 teaspoon vanilla extract

¼ teaspoon kosher salt

¾ cup matzo cake meal

1 cup dried cherries

This rich cake studded with dried cherries will satisfy any chocolate craving. The whipped egg whites keep the texture light and since it's parve, it's great for any occasion, but will definitely be an impressive finish to any seder. **SERVES 6 TO 8**

1 Place one rack in the middle of the oven and another in the bottom third and preheat the oven to 350°F. Line the bottom of a 9-inch springform pan with parchment paper. Grease the inside of the pan and the parchment with margarine.

2 Melt the chocolate and margarine in a small pot over low heat, stirring constantly with a rubber spatula, until smooth. Remove the pot from the heat and set aside to cool slightly.

3 In a stand mixer or in a medium bowl with a whisk, beat the egg whites to stiff peaks. Set aside. In a large bowl, combine the egg yolks, sugar, vanilla, and salt. Beat the mixture until pale and doubled in volume. Add in the chocolate mixture and mix until fully incorporated, scraping down the sides with a rubber spatula to blend evenly. Add the cake meal.

Fold in the egg whites in three batches until evenly incorporated. Fold in the cherries and pour the cake batter into the prepared pan, using the rubber spatula to smooth the top of the cake.

4 Place the cake on the middle rack of the oven and a small pan filled with water on the bottom rack, below the cake. Bake until the cake begins to pull away from the sides of the pan and a wooden skewer inserted in the middle comes out mostly clean with a small amount of fudge and crumb, 35 to 40 minutes. Don't worry if the cake has cracked a bit during baking.

5 Remove the cake from the oven and set on a cooling rack. Allow to cool completely in the springform pan, about 1 hour. When the cake is cool, release the outer ring and invert the cake onto a plate. Slice and serve.

TIP Placing a pan of water in the oven helps keep the cake moist as it evaporates during baking. Just be sure there is enough water to last the whole baking time.

ACKNOWLEDGMENTS

Thank you to Yfat Reiss Gendell, agent extraodinaire, for your enthusiasm, great ideas, and, of course, for making this book happen. Thank you to our editor, Amanda Englander, for helping us stay focused and refining our vision. To the rest of the Clarkson Potter team—Danielle Daitch, Stephanie Huntwork, Sonia Persad, Heather Williamson, Amy Boorstein, Kelli Tokos, and Natasha Martin—thank you for bringing this book to life. You have helped us both fulfill a dream.

To the incredibly talented photographer Jennifer May; the prop guru Barb Fritz; and skillful food stylist Derek Laughern—thank you for your hard work and dedication to making this book as beautiful as it can be.

FROM MIKIE

It has been a pleasure working with David Kirschner. Your commitment, hard work, and care have made this possible. Thank you! To Rabbi Kirshner, thank you for your knowledge, time, and guidance. Wendy Gaynor, amazing chef and instructor, thank you for always inspiring me and for helping me research some of these recipes. To my coaches: Amy Cohen, thank you for your voice, guidance, and humor. Laura Wolf-Slovin, thank you for the direction you are always there to give. There aren't many truer friends.

To the two women I most enjoy eating with: Rebecka Jerome, to think it started all those years ago at our infamous lunch at the Four Seasons. We were so close to having to do those dishes. It's been a lifetime together, and I'm so grateful to share such a rich history with you. Sister Lone, we've had too many great meals to name—Noma! (OK, I had to.) Thank you for all that you have given me. He really did pick you for me. I will always be proud of my Danish heritage.

To the rest of my wonderful family of friends, so much of the happiness I've had has been because of your support, care, and love. Each one of you has given me something so special. Thank you!

My most loving thanks to Joey Heilbrun, both of you, my dad and my daughter. The love I feel for you is boundless.

Finally to the Streits, all of you: past, present, and future generations. What a legacy! May it continue for many years, and may we all make Aron proud.

FROM DAVID

Thank you, Mikie, for trusting me to take on this project with you. It's been an amazing experience working with you to honor your family and the product that they have perfected over so many years. I truly value your friendship and the passion you brought to this book.

To my wife, Allison, thank you for understanding all of my long nights cooking and typing. You are the best friend and partner anybody could wish for. Our life together is the most important thing to me and you inspire me to be the best I can every day.

To my parents, Ira and Joanne, just simply . . . thank you. Nothing I have achieved would've been possible without your love, support, and guidance all these years. Growing up kosher was a special, unique experience that was invaluable to me while writing this book. You kept Judaism present in our home every day, instilling the traditions and values that help make me who I am.

To my family, Pete, Sara, Lisa, Dylan, Aunt Sheila, Allan, Ilyse, Terry, Jason, Stephanie, Dylan, and Emma; and my closest friends, the Barbanels, Bergers, JAG, Lisches, and Schwartzes, I am who I am because of all of you. I will always be grateful for everything you have given me in life. Last, to my late brother Matt, I carry you with me every day. The lessons you taught me, the memories we shared, the type of man you were is what I strive to be. The fight and drive you had is what continues to push me through all the long days of juggling cooking, writing, and life. MEKStrong . . .

INDEX

Note: Page references in *italics* indicate photographs.

Apple Crumb Pie, *104*, 105–6
Avocado(s)
    Matzo Nachos with Pickled Jalapeños, *48*, 49
    and Slow-Roasted Tomato Toasts, *60*, 64

Basil
    Pesto Caprese Matzo Pizza, 74
Beef
    Anytime Brisket with Matzo Spaetzle, *78*, 79–80
    Matzo Tacos with Yesterday's Brisket, *82*, 83
    Meat Loaf with Charred-Tomato Glaze, 91
Blintzes, Blueberry and Cheese, 23–25, *24*
Blueberry and Cheese Blintzes, 23–25, *24*
Broccoli, Potato, and Matzo Gratin, *52*, 53
Butter, 14

Candy
    Chocolate Caramel Matzo Crunch with Candied Ginger, 94, *95*
    Rocky Road Truffles, *96*, 97
Caramel
    Chocolate Matzo Crunch with Candied Ginger, 94, *95*
    Salted, Toasts, *63*, 65
Cheese
    and Blueberry Blintzes, 23–25, *24*
    Cheesy Lemon Pancakes, *18*, 19
    Greek Matzo Panzanella, 42, *43*
    Homemade Ricotta, 20, *20*
    Matzo Chilaquiles, 26, 27
    Matzo Nachos with Pickled Jalapeños, *48*, 49

Matzo Spanakopita, 75–76, 77
Matzo Tiramisu, 102, *103*
Pesto Caprese Matzo Pizza, 74
Potato, Broccoli, and Matzo Gratin, *52*, 53
Whipped Cream, Cucumber, Radish and Watercress Toasts, *60*, 64
White Matzo Pizza with Potatoes and Smoked Gruyère, 72–73, *73*
Cherry(ies)
    -Chocolate Torte, 107
    Matzo Granola, 22
    and Pear Matzo Kugel, *58*, 59
Chicken
    Charred Lemon Braised, 70–71
    Easy Chopped Liver with Pickled Onions, 44
    Fried, Lower East Side, *68*, 69
    Soup, Classic, with Matzo Balls, 32–34, *33*
    -Stuffed Whole-Wheat Matzo Balls in Thyme-Mushroom Broth, 35–36
Chilaquiles, Matzo, 26, 27
Chocolate
    Caramel Matzo Crunch with Candied Ginger, 94, *95*
    -Cherry Torte, 107
    Chip Cookies, 98, *99*
    Ganache, Mexican, Toasts, *62*, 65
    Matzo, Ice Cream Sandwich with, *62*, 65
    Matzo S'mores, *63*, 65
    Matzo Tiramisu, 102, *103*
    Peanut Butter Cup Toasts, *63*, 65
    Rocky Road Truffles, *96*, 97
Citrus juice, 14
Cod Cakes with Remoulade Sauce, 88–90, *89*
Coffee
    Matzo Tiramisu, 102, *103*

Cookies
    Chocolate Chip, 98, *99*
    Pizzarelle, *100*, 101
Cucumber(s)
    Greek Matzo Panzanella, 42, *43*
    Whipped Cream Cheese, Radish and Watercress Toasts, *60*, 64

Dill Yogurt, *55*, 56

Eggs, 13
    L.E.O. Matzo Brei, 28, 29
    Matzo Chilaquiles, 26, 27
    Scrambled, and Crispy Salami Toasts, *60*, 64

Falafel, Quinoa, with Spiced Yogurt Sauce, 84, *85*
Farfel
    about, 13
    Charred Lemon Braised Chicken, 70–71
    Matzo Granola, 22
    Moroccan Matzo Stuffing, 57
    Papa Pomodoro (Tuscan Tomato Matzo Soup), 38, *39*
    Potato, Broccoli, and Matzo Gratin, *52*, 53
    Rocky Road Truffles, *96*, 97
Fish. *See* Cod; Salmon; Whitefish

Ginger, Candied, Chocolate Caramel Matzo Crunch with, 94, *95*
Granola, Matzo, 22
Greens
    Caesar Salad with Smoked Whitefish and Matzo Ball Croutons, *40*, 41
    Greek Matzo Panzanella, 42, *43*
    Matzo Spanakopita, 75–76, 77
    Quinoa Falafel with Spiced Yogurt Sauce, 84, *85*

Herbs, for recipes, 14

Kosher guidelines, 12
Kugel, Pear and Cherry Matzo, *58*, 59

Latkes, Zucchini, with Dill Yogurt, 54, *55*
Lemon Pancakes, Cheesy, *18*, 19
L.E.O. Matzo Brei, 28, 29
Liver, Easy Chopped, with Pickled Onions, 44
Lox. *See under* Salmon

Margarine, 14
Marshmallows
    Matzo S'mores, *63*, 65
    Rocky Road Truffles, *96*, 97
Matzo cake meal
    about, 13
    Apple Crumb Pie, *104*, 105–6
    Cheesy Lemon Pancakes, *18*, 19
    Chocolate-Cherry Torte, 107
    Chocolate Chip Cookies, 98, *99*
    Lower East Side Fried Chicken, *68*, 69
    Matzo Spaetzle, *78*, 80
    Quinoa Falafel with Spiced Yogurt, 84, *85*
Matzo farfel. *See* Farfel
Matzo meal
    about, 13
    Blueberry and Cheese Blintzes, 23–25, *24*
    Caesar Salad with Smoked Whitefish and Matzo Ball Croutons, *40*, 41
    Chicken-Stuffed Whole-Wheat Matzo Balls in Thyme-Mushroom Broth, 35–36
    Chocolate Chip Cookies, 98, *99*
    Classic Chicken Soup with Matzo Balls, 32–34, *33*
    Cod Cakes with Remoulade Sauce, 88–90, *89*

Lower East Side Fried Chicken, 68, 69
Matzo Mustard–Crusted Salmon, 86, 87
Matzo Tacos with Yesterday's Brisket, 82, 83
Meat Loaf with Charred-Tomato Glaze, 91
Pizzarelle, 100, 101
Quinoa Falafel with Spiced Yogurt Sauce, 84, 85
Zucchini Latkes with Dill Yogurt, 54, 55
Matzo sheets
Chocolate Caramel Matzo Crunch with Candied Ginger, 94, 95
Easy Chopped Liver with Pickled Onions, 44
Greek Matzo Panzanella, 42, 43
L.E.O. Matzo Brei, 28, 29
Matzo Chilaquiles, 26, 27
Matzo Nachos with Pickled Jalapeños, 48, 49
Matzo Spanakopita, 75–76, 77
Matzo Tiramisu, 102, 103
Papa Pomodoro (Tuscan Tomato Matzo Soup), 38, 39
Pear and Cherry Matzo Kugel, 58, 59
Pesto Caprese Matzo Pizza, 74
Savory Toasts, 60–61, 64
Sweet Toasts, 62–63, 65
White Matzo Pizza with Potatoes and Smoked Gruyère, 72–73, 73
Meat Loaf with Charred-Tomato Glaze, 91
Mushroom-Thyme Broth, Chicken-Stuffed Whole-Wheat Matzo Balls in, 35–36

Nachos, Matzo, with Pickled Jalapeños, 48, 49

Nuts. See also Pine nuts; Pistachios
Matzo Granola, 22
Pizzarelle, 100, 101
Rocky Road Truffles, 96, 97

Oils, 14
Onions
L.E.O. Matzo Brei, 28, 29
Pickled, 45

Pancakes, Cheesy Lemon, 18, 19
Passover
ingredients, 13–14
kitchen equipment, 14–15
Seder rituals, 9–11
Peanut Butter Cup Toasts, 63, 65
Pear and Cherry Matzo Kugel, 58, 59
Pepper, freshly ground, 14
Peppers
Pickled Jalapeños, 50
Salsa Verde, 26, 27
Pesto Caprese Matzo Pizza, 74
Pickled Jalapeños, 50
Pickled Onions, 45
Pie, Apple Crumb, 104, 105–6
Pine nuts
Matzo Spanakopita, 75–76, 77
Pesto Caprese Matzo Pizza, 74
Pizzarelle, 100, 101
Pistachios
Matzo Granola, 22
Moroccan Matzo Stuffing, 57
Pizza
Pesto Caprese Matzo, 74
White Matzo, with Potatoes and Smoked Gruyère, 72–73, 73
Pizzarelle, 100, 101
Potato(es)
Broccoli, and Matzo Gratin, 52, 53
Cod Cakes with Remoulade Sauce, 88–90, 89

and Smoked Gruyère, White Matzo Pizza with, 72–73, 73
Potato starch, about, 13

Quinoa Falafel with Spiced Yogurt Sauce, 84, 85

Raisins
Matzo Granola, 22
Moroccan Matzo Stuffing, 57
Pizzarelle, 100, 101
Rocky Road Truffles, 96, 97

Salads
Caesar, with Smoked Whitefish and Matzo Ball Croutons, 40, 41
Greek Matzo Panzanella, 42, 43
Salami, Crispy, and Scrambled Eggs Toasts, 60, 64
Salmon
L.E.O. Matzo Brei, 28, 29
Lox, Lemon Yogurt, Capers, and Dill Toasts, 61, 64
Matzo Mustard–Crusted, 86, 87
Salsa Verde, 26, 27
Salt, 13
Sauces
Remoulade, 89, 90
Salsa Verde, 26, 27
Spiced Yogurt, 85, 85
Scallion, Charred, Dip Toasts, 61, 64
Schmaltz, 14
Soups
Chicken, Classic, with Matzo Balls, 32–34, 33
Chicken-Stuffed Whole-Wheat Matzo Balls in Thyme-Mushroom Broth, 35–36
Tomato Matzo, Tuscan (Papa Pomodoro), 38, 39
Spaetzle, Matzo, 78, 80
Spanakopita, Matzo, 75–76, 77

Spinach
Matzo Spanakopita, 75–76, 77
Stuffing, Moroccan Matzo, 57

Tacos, Matzo, with Yesterday's Brisket, 82, 83
Tiramisu, Matzo, 102, 103
Tomatillos
Salsa Verde, 26, 27
Tomato(es)
Charred-, Glaze, Meat Loaf with, 91
Greek Matzo Panzanella, 42, 43
Matzo Nachos with Pickled Jalapeños, 48, 49
Matzo Soup, Tuscan (Papa Pomodoro), 38, 39
Pesto Caprese Matzo Pizza, 74
Slow-Roasted, and Avocado Toasts, 60, 64
Torte, Chocolate-Cherry, 107
Truffles, Rocky Road, 96, 97

Whitefish, Smoked, and Matzo Ball Croutons, Caesar Salad with, 40, 41

Yogurt
Dill, 55, 56
Lemon, Lox, Capers, and Dill Toasts, 61, 64
Sauce, Spiced, 85, 85

Zucchini Latkes with Dill Yogurt, 54, 55

ABOUT THE AUTHORS

MIKIE HEILBRUN is a fourth-generation Streit. Born in Brooklyn and raised in Manhattan, she is a very recent transplant to Savannah, Georgia. Mikie spent more than twenty-five years as a casting director and the last few as the proud mother of her daughter, Joey.

DAVID KIRSCHNER is a Michelin-trained chef who has spent fifteen years working in and running some of the country's highest-acclaimed restaurants and is the former executive chef for TastingTable.com. He currently runs his own boutique private dining company, dineDK, producing cooking events around the greater New York City area, while continuing to write, food style, and consult on all matters culinary. David resides in Hoboken, New Jersey, with his wife, Allison.